THE TIME HAS
COME...

TO ACCEPT YOUR INTUITIVE

Gifts!

OTHER HAY HOUSE TITLES
BY SONIA CHOQUETTE

Books and Card Decks

The Answer Is Simple . . .
(available September 2008)

The Answer Is Simple Oracle Cards
(available January 2009)

Ask Your Guides

Ask Your Guides Oracle Cards

Diary of a Psychic

The Intuitive Spark

Soul Lessons and Soul Purpose

Soul Lessons and Soul Purpose Oracle Cards

Trust Your Vibes

*Trust Your Vibes at Work, and
Let Them Work for <u>You</u>*

Trust Your Vibes Oracle Cards

Vitamins for the Soul

CD Programs

Attunement to Higher Vibrational Living
(4-CD set), with Mark Stanton Welch

*How to Trust Your Vibes at Work and
Let Them Work for <u>You</u>* (4-CD set)

*Meditations for Receiving Divine Guidance,
Support, and Healing* (2-CD set)

Trust Your Vibes (6-CD set)

THE TIME HAS
COME...

TO ACCEPT YOUR INTUITIVE

Gifts!

SONIA CHOQUETTE

HAY HOUSE, INC.
Carlsbad, California • New York City
London • Sydney • Johannesburg
Vancouver • Hong Kong • New Delhi

Published and distributed in the United States by: Hay House, Inc.:
www.hayhouse.com • **Published and distributed in Australia by:**
Hay House Australia Pty. Ltd.: www.hayhouse.com.au • **Published
and distributed in the United Kingdom by:** Hay House UK, Ltd.:
www.hayhouse.co.uk • **Published and distributed in the Republic
of South Africa by:** Hay House SA (Pty), Ltd.: www.hayhouse.
co.za • **Distributed in Canada by:** Raincoast: www.raincoast.
com • **Published in India by:** Hay House Publishers India: www.
hayhouse.co.in

Editorial supervision: Jill Kramer • *Design:* Tricia Breidenthal

Library of Congress Control Number: 2007930835

ISBN: 978-1-4019-1735-7

11 10 09 08   4 3 2 1
1st edition, April 2008

Printed in the United States of America

A Note from the Author

This book is a personal invitation, from me and other kindred spirits throughout the ages, to accept your sixth sense—your intuition—for the wonderful and essential gift from God that it is.

Intuition is natural; it's trustworthy; and it's indispensable for successfully achieving your hopes, dreams, and heart's desires. You don't have to work to earn intuition—it's the voice of your Spirit, your Divine Essence, and is given to you freely. It's only necessary to open your heart and listen to its quiet and subtle presence deep within.

Intuition holds the key to all you seek in life. Now is the time to accept this Divine gift and allow it to light your way. It will heal you . . . it will heal us all.

(Please note that any entries in the book that do not have a specific identifier included underneath are by me.)

— SONIA

*T*he intuitive mind is a sacred gift and the rational mind its faithful servant. We have created a society that honors the servant and has forgotten the gift.

— ALBERT EINSTEIN

*O*ur intuitive knowing is the gift of our Spirit. The Divine Spirit within each of us illuminates our way, like a light in the dark night. It's our companion, our protector, our moral compass, and our creative genius. Become aware of the Divine Spirit within you, and honor its sacred presence.

Spirit: (noun) the vital principle or animating force within living beings: breath, Divine Spark, force vital

— *The American Heritage Dictionary of the English Language,* Dictionary.com

*E*very human being has, like Socrates, an attendant spirit; and wise are they who obey its signals. If it does not always tell us what to do, it always cautions us what not to do.

— Lydia M. Child

The more you connect with your Spirit and listen for its subtle guidance, the more graceful your life will be, even through the challenges and confusion that meet you along the way.

Just for today, acknowledge and respect every hunch, vibe, bright idea, gut feeling, or intuitive hit that you feel, sense, or experience as an important message from your Divine Spirit, otherwise known as your Higher Self. Then act accordingly.

*I*ntuition is the highest form of knowledge, surpassing both empirical knowledge derived from the senses and scientific knowledge derived from reasoning on the basis of experience.

— BENEDICT DE SPINOZA

*S*tart your morning with this prayer:

Higher Self, Divine Spirit within, guide me through this day. Guide my body. Guide my thoughts. Guide my intentions, conversations, and decisions. I give you full permission to take charge.

Then relax, and rest assured that you're in good care.

*I*ntuition is the counsel coming
from our timeless, boundless
Divine Spirit. It's so large that
it sees beyond all limitations.

*P*erhaps one of the most immediate
rewards of embracing your intuition
is that it's infinitely more clever and
humorous than your ego will ever
be. You'll be highly impressed and
entertained by its offerings.

*A*s soon as you trust yourself,
you will know how to live.

— JOHANN WOLFGANG VON GOETHE

*W*e're endowed by our Creator
with six senses, not five. The sixth
sense is the voice of the Divine Spirit
within, the acceptance of which will
lead us to break through to the next
frontier in human possibility
and creative expression.

$\mathcal{S}$top questioning the sixth sense—it's part of you. Feel it deep down. The real question is not *Do you believe in the sixth sense?* but rather, *Do you believe in <u>you?</u>* When you can say yes, you'll experience your full intuitive genius.

$\mathcal{C}$ommand by instinct is swifter, subtler, deeper, more accurate, more in touch with reality than command by conscious mind. The discovery takes one's breath away.

— MICHAEL NOVAK

*Y*our sixth sense doesn't always communicate through words. Sometimes it simply moves you in the best direction for your highest good. . . . Go with it.

*B*e flexible—in body and mind. That way, when your Spirit moves you in a certain direction, you'll be able to respond.

*W*hen asked, "Do you believe in the sixth sense?" answer without hesitation, "Of course I do—it's my greatest asset, a Divine gift, for which I am forever grateful." And believe it, because it's true.

*I*f we have listening ears, God speaks to us in our own language, whatever that language is.

— MAHATMA GANDHI

Before coming to a decision, make a habit of saying, if only to yourself, *Let me turn this over to my Spirit, my sixth sense, and see what it has to say.* Then do.

The difference between those who live in the blessed flow of intuitive grace and those who live in agonizing fear and regret is simply this: The former act on their intuition, while the latter analyze it to death.

*I*f you accept that you're Divine, your sixth sense makes sense. If you reject your Divinity, then nothing makes sense.

*Y*our Divine Spirit is centered in your heart. That's why listening to your heart is the most important kind of listening you can do.

There's a huge difference between hearing your inner voice and listening to it. To hear yet choose to ignore your Spirit will throw you out of harmony with yourself and into energetic chaos. To hear your inner voice and listen to its wisdom will align you with your Higher Self and empower you with invincible integrity and strength.

It is only with the heart that one can see rightly; what is essential is invisible to the eye.

— ANTOINE DE SAINT-EXUPÉRY

Clairvoyance isn't difficult to
develop. Simply look past appearances
and into the deeper essence of life,
and it will open up to you.

The eyes have sight; the
Spirit has vision. The eyes see
part of the picture; the Spirit
sees the whole picture.

*O*ur sixth sense is our inner radar, our internal barometer, our litmus test within, for truth in life. As Divine Spirit, it guides us through confusion and back to clarity. It assesses the vibrations of the world around us, keeps us grounded, and reveals the truth in all matters. It communicates to us through a silent yet powerful inner voice, arising from the center of the heart. When it speaks, we may not always hear it over the rumble of our mind chatter, but we'll always feel it.

*A*ffirm often and out loud:

"As a Divine Being, I accept all of my spiritual gifts—including my intuition— without resistance or question, and I give thanks for the blessings they bring."

I learned that nothing is impossible
when we follow our inner guidance,
even when its direction may threaten
us by reversing our usual logic.

— GERALD JAMPOLSKY

*T*here are times when intuition
may seem "crazy" or make no
logical sense. This is because the
rational mind is only partly informed.
That's the beauty of the sixth sense:
It reveals what we do not
yet know—but must.

One of the most important reasons to listen to our inner voice, the Divine Spirit within, is to make the best possible choices in life. In keeping with its purpose, when we're on the wrong path or going in the wrong direction, our sixth sense won't hesitate to tell us so.

Don't meet your intuition with suspicion, as though it were an invasive intruder. As the voice of your Higher Self, the Divine Spirit within, greet it with appreciation and respect. Welcome it with an open heart as an honored guest gracing your door.

$\mathcal{Y}$our sixth sense isn't linear, nor
is it always instantly verifiable. Trust
it anyway—it sees what logic can't.

$\mathcal{I}$ntuition, like life, flows. It's not
fixed, static, rigid, or even "right."
It simply reveals, moment to moment,
what is true for now. As the moments
change, so does your inner voice.
Listening to it is like learning to surf.
Feel the waves of life come toward
you, and then use your intuition
to ride them with grace.

*T*here are two aspects to our hearts:

1. We possess the romantic, subjective heart that wants the world to take care of us. This heart is childish and naïve, and it often gets hurt and disappointed by others. It's fickle, restless, insecure, and ungrounded.

2. Then we have the Wise Sage heart. This is the eternal Light of our Spirit. It's calm, grounded, and confident.

Ask the romantic heart to turn to the Wise Sage heart—instead of others—for all that it needs . . . and your life will be sweet, sound, and secure.

. . . [I]t is wisdom to believe the heart.

— GEORGE SANTAYANA

*D*o you welcome the Divine Spirit into your heart? Or do you treat it as though it were an unwelcome squatter that your ego keeps trying to kick out?

*E*mbracing your intuition and choosing to follow your sixth sense as your highest authority is the most personally empowering decision you'll ever make.

*E*very night before retiring, review the day with an eye toward any and all visitations by your Higher Self—your Divine Spirit—however subtle they may have been. Note the presence of your intuition and the messages or insights that it ushered in. Don't search for grand entries. Intuition is low-key and prefers quietly sneaking in the back door of your thoughts. Did you notice?

*T*rust your hunches. They're usually based on facts filed away just below the conscious level.

— DR. JOYCE BROTHERS

*T*hank goodness! Even scientists are catching up with metaphysicians, finally giving us full permission to listen to our Divine Spirit, our inner voice, more respectfully.

*Y*ou know more than you think you know. And you're aware of more than you're consciously tuned in to at any given time. Quiet your ego and your deeper wisdom will surface. *Shh!*

*Y*our Spirit is a messenger of the Great Creator, and its highest purpose is to activate the creative spark within you.

*S*peaking of sparks, you need a little spark to follow your inner voice—it's called courage. Fortunately, this very same spark of courage will also jump-start your creativity, fuel your passion, and bring forth your inner peace as well.

A hunch is creativity trying
to tell you something.

— Anonymous

*N*o matter how subtle, all intuitive
feelings are relevant, even when it's
unclear exactly what your sixth sense is
trying to convey. Believe that the message
important, and be patient as it develops
into meaningful guidance. Meditate and
pray for your hunches to become clear.
Talk them over with a trusted friend
for clarity. With a little attention—and
at times, some more sleuthing—your
hunches will surely develop into full-
blown and clear intuitive direction.

*Y*our Spirit loves to drop in unannounced, like an old and beloved friend. It surprises you with an "Aha," a bright idea, a "hit," a hunch, or a "vibe." Consider yourself fortunate to receive such spontaneous company.

*T*he Divine Spirit within is subtle, pointing the way to opportunities that your ego would never notice. It suggests rather than commands— that's one significant difference between your Spirit and ego.

*W*hen your intuition appears to be sleeping or seems to be nowhere in sight, start singing, dancing, and laughing out loud. This will most certainly wake up your Spirit and call it home to you.

*T*he Spirit is a holy force and requires a clear and loving home within your body. House it properly by taking good care of yourself physically and by keeping your emotions clear of negative debris. If you do so, your Spirit will reside as a Mighty Force within you.

*N*ame your Spirit and have
frequent heart-to-heart conversations.
It's your beloved and trustworthy
teacher and friend.

*B*elief consists in accepting
the affirmations of the soul;
unbelief, in denying them.

— RALPH WALDO EMERSON

*Y*our sixth sense serves to guide your choices and especially to correct those leading you in the wrong direction. A warning from the Higher Self is a blessing, sent to keep you from veering off your soul's path.

*W*hen the Divine Spirit within gifts you with intuitive flashes and insights (even ones that are difficult to accept), don't forget your manners. Always say "Thank you."

*I*ntuition arises most often in an organized and prepared mind. When seeking guidance on something, first become as soundly informed as you can, then turn it over. Your conscious mind and your Spirit are meant to be great creative partners.

*I*ntuition is only given to him who has gone through long preparation to receive it.

— Louis Pasteur

*I*f the mind is engaged in soulless concerns—filling itself with gossip, blame, criticism, voyeurism, negativity, self-abuse, or abuse of others—it disconnects fully and absolutely from the Higher Self, your Divine Spirit. These foolish preoccupations are toxic to the Spirit and death to intuition.

*T*o set up continual receptive rapport with your Higher Self, become clear and focused on what you want to be guided about. The clearer you are in your intentions, the more your Divine Spirit can assist you.

Place an INTUITION IS RESPECTED HERE sign on your desk in your office and in your home. It will both speak for itself and serve as a reminder to you.

The Universe isn't random, although it may appear to be, and neither is your intuition. Your inner voice responds to a genuine desire to know the truth. It assembles, compiles, synthesizes, distills, and assimilates information from many resources in order to offer you direction. Be clear what you seek and your Spirit will provide guidance.

Good instincts tell you what
to do long before your
head has figured it out.

— MICHAEL BURKE

Don't overrate your ego. It's never
as well informed as your Spirit.

An intuitive insight is almost always better than any answer your ego could come up with on its own.

Don't ever try to convince someone else to respect your intuition—that's your job.

The best way to respect your intuition is to quietly but firmly embrace its wisdom and act from there, without allowing interference from others.

Intuition is subtle and can be shy, but it thrives on joy and happiness. Coax it in through play, humor, laughter, and wonder. Dedicate yourself to having fun in life and intuition will be your constant playmate.

$\mathcal{T}$hank goodness you aren't limited
to what your intellect alone knows.
The mind is subjective, biased,
opinionated, argumentative,
ill informed, insecure, and quite
often confused. The Divine Spirit
within is clear, direct, efficient,
confident, and truthful.

$\mathcal{I}$f the doors of perception were
cleansed, every thing would appear
to man as it is, infinite.

For man has closed himself up, till he
sees all things thro' narrow
chinks of his cavern.

— WILLIAM BLAKE

*N*ever assume that what you know is all there is to know. Your intuition will quickly relieve you of this delusion.

*D*on't allow a negative or critical viewpoint to keep you from seeing the truth with your intuitive eye. Keep the lens of your perspective clear by looking at life with appreciation, acceptance, interest, and love. Doing so will sharpen your intuitive sight and reveal possibilities that you never knew existed.

To keep your viewpoint clear, meditate. Retreat from the noisy world for a few minutes every day and go within. Contemplate God, but don't make this too complicated. It's not a punishment for the ego—it's a vacation from it.

To meditate is a self-empowering choice. Make it simple: Sit quietly for five minutes a day and merely focus on your breathing. When inhaling, mentally say *I am . . .* and on the exhale, say *peaceful.* If your mind drifts, don't stress or worry about it. Simply refocus and concentrate on your breath once again, repeating *I am . . .* on the inhale and *peaceful* on the exhale. Gradually extend the 5 minutes to 10, then to 15—that's enough for a successful meditation period. As you breathe in, imagine the oxygen refreshing your blood cells, invigorating your lungs, feeding your muscles and nerve endings, and nurturing every part of your body. Do this in place of a coffee break—it will be far more effective in connecting you to your Spirit and fueling your creative fires.

*B*e flexible in every way—in mind, body, and emotion. Intuition is a subtle force that seeks to move you toward your highest good. Your part is to be flexible enough to be moved when your intuition speaks.

*Y*our intuition will never try to control you; it will only point the way. If you choose to ignore it or go in another direction, *you* cause the problem—not your intuition.

*B*efriend the Divine Spirit within and trust its influence. It's the most devoted, reliable, and stubbornly loving friend you'll ever have, so stop giving it such a hard time!

*T*he more you embrace your intuition as a positive force in your life, the more it will become so.

It is by logic that we prove, but by
intuition that we discover.

— HENRI POINCARÉ

Don't allow others to rob
you of your confidence in your
inner voice with their confusion
and pseudoscientific biases. True
scientists acknowledge and respect
intuition as their greatest resource,
aware that the sixth sense leads the
way in all discoveries. If great men
and women know this and say
so, you can trust in it as well.

*W*hen it comes to life, we've been conditioned to follow the "rules." We haven't been encouraged to abide by the Divine Spirit within. There are times when following the rules is a smart decision, such as when driving in traffic. But then there are occasions when following the "rules" will simply sweep you into mass mind confusion and congestion. When it comes to driving your car, follow the rules. When it comes to living your life, follow your Spirit.

*T*here are no rules.
Just follow your heart.

— ROBIN WILLIAMS

*E*very time I've done
something that doesn't feel right,
it's ended up not being right.

— MARIO CUOMO

*I*f others dismiss or invalidate your
intuition, just realize that their egos
are feeling threatened. Don't allow
this to intimidate you. The same
holds true if *you* find fault with or
hesitate to trust your own intuition.
Breathe through your doubt and
the temptation to ignore this wisdom,
and embrace your inner voice anyway.

Respect your inner signals
no matter how uncomfortable
and disruptive to your and others'
plans they may be. A temporary
inconvenience is far easier to
adjust to than a mistake
you were warned about.

Your vision will become clear
only when you look into your
heart. . . . Who looks outside,
dreams. Who looks inside, awakens.

— CARL JUNG

The world is confusing; your Spirit is not. The opinions of others are confusing; the wisdom of your inner voice is not.

Don't let the swirling energies of the world overwhelm your Spirit. Step back, detach, find your center, and go within. What you seek will always be found there.

A great many people think they
are thinking when they are merely
rearranging their prejudices.

— WILLIAM JAMES

*Y*our intuition cuts through the layers
of assumption that you were handed
along the way as truth and points
you toward what's genuine, real,
and authentic for you.

Only intuition can save you from
the most dangerous individual of
them all, the articulate incompetent.

— ROBERT BERNSTEIN

There will always be someone
who presents himself as the "expert."
Beware. Listen, consider, ask questions,
and then turn it over to the only
genuinely reliable expert
for you . . . your Spirit.

*M*odern man's besetting temptation
is to sacrifice his direct perceptions
and spontaneous feelings to his reasoned
reflections; to prefer in all circumstances
the verdict of his intellect to that
of his immediate intuitions.

— ALDOUS HUXLEY

*T*he time has come to elevate the
status of the sixth sense, your inner
wisdom and authentic knowing, from the
lost, ignored sense to the first and most
important of them all. No longer allow
your intuition to be the "throwaway" or
dispensable sense that disturbs your ego's
tight control. To lose your instincts—
or abandon them to the least important
of influences—is an error for which
you'll almost certainly pay dearly.

*O*ne of the reasons why so
few of us act, rather than react,
is because we are continually
stifling our deepest impulses.

— Henry Miller

*W*hen confused, uninspired, lost,
or insecure, start naming out loud—
without any rhyme or reason—
what is true for you right now. This
includes what you enjoy, what makes
you laugh, what annoys you, what
attracts or repels you . . . in other
words, whatever speaks to your Spirit.
When you acknowledge freely what
speaks to your Spirit, it begins
to speak freely to you.

*U*nless intuition builds the house,
they labor in vain who build it.

— FLORENCE SCOVEL SHINN

*B*eware of those who deny the
magic of Spirit. They've lost touch
with the Infinite and are caught
up in the isolation of their futile,
ego-driven existence. In their misery,
they seek your company.

*I*f you let your fear of consequence prevent you from following your deepest instinct then your life will be safe, expedient and thin.

— KATHERINE BUTLER HATHAWAY

*Y*es, it's at times frightening to follow your intuition, but considering the alternative, it's far more frightening not to.

I go by instinct. . . .
I don't worry about experience.

— BARBRA STREISAND

*T*he natural world has its own wisdom.
Trees blossom. Birds and butterflies
migrate. Whales cross oceans. Penguins
march across tundras. All find their way
to their greatest flowering by cooperating
with their instincts. We're part of the
natural world as well—no different. If we
would only flow with our own instincts as
the rest of the natural world does, we, too,
would experience our greatest flowering.

The Divine Spirit within protects,
but it doesn't interfere. It warns,
but it doesn't intrude. It guides,
but it doesn't impose. It waits
for you . . . but it is patient.

And ye shall know the truth,
and the truth shall make you free.

— JESUS (JOHN 8:32)

Intuition means "inner teacher."
Our inner teacher, our Spirit, serves
always and only to reveal the truth.
The choice to listen is ours.

We each need to let our intuition
guide us and then be willing to follow
that guidance directly and fearlessly.

— SHAKTI GAWAIN

Choosing to follow the Divine Spirit within as your Highest Authority is a bold and brave act of defiance— rebelling against control, fear, and a haunting sense of inadequacy.

He who marches joyfully in rank and file has already earned my contempt. He has been a given a large brain by mistake, since for him, a spinal column would suffice.

— ALBERT EINSTEIN

*S*eeking the approval of others
over that which comes from within
is a death sentence to your intuition—
and to your life. Never set such
store by something as worthless and
destructive to your Spirit as blindly
following outward, rather than
boldly going inward.

*W*hen I've been most effective,
I've listened to my inner voice.

— NORMAN LEAR

$\mathcal{D}$on't dilute your inner voice
by soliciting the opinions of others,
heeding them over its counsel. Why
ask mere mortals for advice when
you're guided by Sacred Wisdom.
Treasure your sixth sense. Treat
it like gold. Wear it close to your
heart, and don't allow anyone
to rob you of its power.

$\mathcal{I}$t isn't difficult to trust your
inner voice. Just pay attention to
its counsel and notice the results of
your listening . . . or not. This should
provide ample evidence that
your trust isn't misplaced.

*H*ave you ever observed how
endlessly seeking advice from others
is mostly a way for you to deny or
ignore your own intuition? Have you
also noticed how this doesn't work?

*T*he Holy Spirit will always guide
you truly, for your joy is his.

— *A Course in Miracles*

*O*ur Creator provides us—as Divine Beings, children of the Most High—with all we need to grow, thrive, succeed, create, enjoy, and take pleasure in life. He gives us a magical garden to play in here on Earth; but to enter the magic requires a certain key: your intuition, which can be found in your heart.

A trembling in the bones may carry a more convincing testimony than the dry deduction of the brain.

— LLEWELLYN POWERS

The Divine Spirit within is a fiery force. Most times it's a quiet-glowing ember, but occasionally it can become a lightning bolt.

The ego-mind can be quite the bully, imposing itself as the final authority. The body, however, pays it no heed, remaining forever faithful to the true authority of Spirit.

*T*he high-minded man must
care more for the truth than
what people think.

— ARISTOTLE

*N*ever impose your intuition on
anyone as the truth . . . only gently
but firmly introduce it as *your* truth.

*T*his immediate access to Truth is
the ultimate destiny of all human
beings, and it seems probable that
some day the mind itself will lie
as much below the threshold of
consciousness as the instincts now do.

— ALICE BAILEY

*T*he more we accept our destiny
as Divine Beings, the more easily we
can converse with God. It is through
our hearts that we speak to our
Higher Power, and intuition
is God speaking to us.

*T*he intuitive eye focuses like a hawk. It zeros in on the essential— the authentic—and ignores the rest.

*I*ntuition is the undoubting conception of a pure and attentive mind, which arises from the light of reason alone, and is more certain even than deduction.

— RENÉ DESCARTES

*I*ntuition doesn't compete with reason—it complements it. They're natural partners and are designed to work together. The key to their compatibility, however, is not to confuse the faculty of reason—also a gift from Spirit—with the blathering of the ego, which bears no gift at all.

*P*art of the brain may be able to sense danger and provide early warnings to help humans escape, according to a new study that provides new evidence of the brain's "sixth sense."

— FROM A WEBMD ARTICLE
(FEBRUARY 17, 2005)
www.webmd.com

$\mathcal{A}$nyone who doesn't accept or believe in the legitimacy of intuition today isn't fully informed in the modern world. Don't allow yourself to be one of those people.

$\mathcal{T}$rust your instincts. Act on them.

— SETH GRODIN

It's not enough to sense your intuition. It's only when you embrace and act on its guidance that it will make a powerful and protective difference in your life.

When it comes to intuition, don't hesitate to listen: Its greatest power lies in the moment it presents itself.

*W*e think of intuition as not rigorous, as all about some weird unfathomable emotion. But I take it much more seriously than that.

— MALCOLM GLADWELL

*I*ntuition only *appears* to be random, when in fact on the energetic plane its wisdom arises from perfectly mathematical intersections. Just because our conscious minds don't comprehend or see all the elements converging at once to offer up our most profound insights doesn't make them any less intelligent or exact.

intuition: (noun) the immediate
knowing or learning of something
without the conscious use of reasoning

— WEBSTER'S NEW WORLD DICTIONARY

We're hardwired into the quantum
field, not simply as observers, but as
part of all there is. We know things
intuitively because they're intimately
part of us. We only appear to be
separate or alone. Intuition
reminds us that we're not.

*Y*ou have to leave the city of your comfort and go into the wilderness of your intuition . . . what you'll discover will be wonderful. What you'll discover will be yourself.

— ALAN ALDA

*Y*es, it can feel intimidating, reckless, irresponsible, and even dangerous to follow the path where your Spirit beckons you. However, you'll discover that if you breathe into your resistance and fear, it turns into adventure.

*N*o matter what you are doing,
ask for guidance. It saves time and
energy and often a lifetime of misery.

— FLORENCE SCOVEL SHINN

*B*etter yet is trusting and then
acting on the guidance you receive.
Your Higher Self, the Divine Spirit
within, resonates with all that
is harmonious and in Divine
Order, leading you from chaos
into balance and peace.

*Y*our Higher Self, your Divine Spirit within, knows that the most valuable thing you have is time, and it serves to help you use it in the most efficient, effective, and energizing way possible.

*W*e denote this primary wisdom as Intuition, whilst all later teachings are tuitions.

— RALPH WALDO EMERSON

*W*hat you know intellectually is acquired from others. What you know intuitively you receive from God.

*I*ntuition doesn't necessarily tell you what's going to happen, but it will always guide you in how best to respond no matter what *does* happen.

$\mathcal{L}$istening to the inner voice—
trusting the inner voice—is one of the
most important lessons of leadership.

— WARREN BENNIS

$\mathcal{I}$f you do not express your own
original ideas, if you do not listen
to your own being, you will
have betrayed yourself.

— ROLLO MAY

To claim your power, be authentic.
To be authentic, listen to your Spirit.

If . . . you align with love . . . then
you'll be led by the voice of intuition.

— STEVE PAVLINA

*L*ove fuels intuition. The more
you love, the more you'll feel
the presence and power of your
Spirit guiding your life.

*B*e who you are and say what
you feel, because those who
mind don't matter and those
who matter don't mind.

— DR. SEUSS

The most compelling reason to listen to and follow your intuition is that it's so darned uncomfortable not to.

Seek not from without, but to those consciousnesses, those voices, those feelings, those vibrations as may arise from within. For know, as has been indicated, there He, the Giver of all good and perfect gifts, makes to grow those seeds which ye have sown.

— EDGAR CAYCE

*I*n the center of your heart lies a door
to heaven. As you open it, you're met
with hosts of heavenly helpers ready
to serve and guide you. You must go
deep within, to the core of your being,
however, to find the door. It can't be
entered through the intellect and will
never be found through others.

*T*his above all, to
thine own self be true.

— WILLIAM SHAKESPEARE

And know the true self *is* your Spirit.

It is the heart which experiences
God, not the reason.

— BLAISE PASCAL

The sixth sense is a faculty of the Divine Spirit, not of the intellect. It's an artistic, creative, soulful expression. To connect with the sixth sense is an art.

A good artist lets his intuition lead him wherever it wants.

— LAO-TZU

*A*ll great men are gifted with
intuition. They know without
reasoning or analysis what
they need to know.

— ALEXIS CARREL

*S*top defending or explaining
your intuition to others, especially
when you know that they aren't
open to your explanations anyway.
Don't require that your intuition be
authenticated by others. Respect and
honor it as your *own* authentic voice.

*I*ntuition comes very close to
clairvoyance; it appears to be the
extrasensory perception of reality.

— ALEXIS CARREL

*I*t's interesting how some people
are comfortable with the word *intuition,*
but heaven forbid you cross that line
and call it something more, such as
clairvoyance! That spooks! Yet when
you think about it, your intuition,
when finely tuned, becomes extremely
clairvoyant, which means "clear seeing."
It also becomes clairaudient, or clear
hearing, and clairsentient, clear
feeling. In fact, the more you use it,
the more *everything* becomes clear.

$\mathcal{T}$he only real valuable
thing is intuition.

— ALBERT EINSTEIN

$\mathcal{I}$f you were to lose all your five sense
faculties but still had your intuition,
you'd be safe and find your way.
If you have all five sense faculties
but lose connection with your
intuition, you'll be completely lost.

*Intuition is the clear concept
of the whole at once.*

— JOHANN KASPAR LAVATER

As Divine Beings, we're
connected, through our Spirit,
to the quantum field. With
meditation, practice, intense
inquiry, and quiet introspection,
we can tap into this field and get
our answers directly from God.

*I*ntuition is the supra-logic that cuts
out all routine processes of thought
and leaps straight from the
problem to the answer.

— ROBERT GRAVES

*I*ntuition saves time.

The mind can assert anything, and pretend it has proved it. My beliefs I test on my body, on my intuitional consciousness, and when I get a response there, then I accept.

— D. H. LAWRENCE

The body tells the truth because Divine Spirit flows through it. Therefore, listen to your physical self when you seek confirmation. If something is correct, supportive, right, and true for you, your body will be relaxed and peaceful. If it doesn't feel at ease with something, that thing is simply wrong.

$\mathcal{L}$isten to your intuition. It will tell you everything you need to know.

— Anthony J. D'Angelo

$\mathcal{Y}$ou're never alone and never without direction. It's just necessary to look within.

*T*alk sense to a fool and
he calls you foolish.

— EURIPIDES

*I*s it really so painful to have people
dismiss your intuition? Apparently
it isn't if you're Einstein, Aristotle,
Edison, Copernicus, the Wright
brothers, Henry Ford, or Bill Gates,
to name a few creative geniuses.
At least if people laugh at you,
you're in better company than
those who are laughing!

*O*nly ask the opinion of those whom you not only admire, but who have actually succeeded in what you seek to accomplish. Inevitably they'll lead you back to you and your truth, because it's what worked for them.

*W*e should take care not to make the intellect our god; it has, of course, powerful muscles, but no personality.

— ALBERT EINSTEIN

One of the ego's deepest fears is that we're not considered "smart enough," so we trick ourselves into believing that knowing and reciting facts and opinions enhances our intelligence in the eyes of others. In fact, all this does is create mental congestion that bogs down the brain and disconnects us from our deepest wisdom. To be truly intelligent, obtain accurate facts, as they're relevant; discriminate when it comes to opinions; and in the end, turn everything over to your Higher Self, your Spirit, for answers.

Trust the instinct to the end, though you can render no reason.

— RALPH WALDO EMERSON

$\mathcal{S}$top thinking so much and listen within. You'll be shown what you must know next.

$\mathcal{L}$et's simply stop explaining or defending our sixth sense to anyone. It's a gift from God—one that we must honor and respect. Have compassion for those who've lost *their* gift, but don't try to keep them comfortable by distancing yourself from your own.

*O*nce you get rid of the idea that you must please other people before you please yourself, and you begin to follow your instincts—only then can you be satisfied. You become more satisfied, and when you are, other people will tend to be satisfied by what you do.

— RAQUEL WELCH

*H*ere's an interesting paradox: Many refuse to acknowledge their sixth sense and deepest intuition for fear they'll lose the respect of others . . . yet it's those who *embrace* their sixth sense and inner knowing till the end who gain our highest respect.

I make all decisions on intuition. I throw a spear into the darkness. That is my intuition. Then I must send an army into the darkness to find the spear. That is the intellect.

— INGMAR BERGMAN

*T*o follow your sixth sense takes courage. You can't play it safe and play it true at the same time. However, to assume that following your Spirit will cause chaos is shortsighted and presumptuous. It may create colossal inconvenience for a brief while, but it actually restores order, harmony, and beauty and brings a positive solution in the end.

*F*acts . . . are not truths; they are not conclusions; they are not even premisses, but in the nature and parts of the premisses.

— SAMUEL TAYLOR COLERIDGE

*T*he fact is, intuition is real, so it's folly to ignore, denounce, diminish, argue with, or doubt its value. Another fact is, those who do ignore, diminish, or argue with their intuition doubt their Spirit— that's a sad but true fact.

*F*acts are true . . . as of yesterday.
Tomorrow they may change because
of the discoveries of today.

*O*ften you have to rely on intuition.

— BILL GATES

*W*hen you run out of answers and have no clues, you don't have to come to a dead end. Go inward—your Spirit will step in and guide you, because it's connected to Divine Source. When the intellect is out of ideas, ask your Spirit, for its supply of answers is never exhausted.

*I*t is always with excitement that I wake up in the morning wondering what my intuition will toss up at me, like gifts from the sea. I work with it and rely on it. It's my partner.

— Dr. Jonas Salk

$\mathcal{S}$tart each morning by affirming the Divine Spirit within. Ask that it lead you throughout the day. Keep your heart open to its guidance, and have the courage to follow its promptings when you feel them.

$\mathcal{E}$mbrace your intuition as your dearest friend—look forward to its input. Allow for it. Seek it. Count on it. Know that it will be there for you, filled with surprises, gifts, and contributions. Greet your Spirit every morning, consult with it throughout the day, and thank it before you go to bed.

One definition of *intuition* is "to pay attention"; another is "to notice." To sharpen your intuition, slow down and pay attention to what's around you right now. Notice sounds, shapes, colors, and objects. Better yet, announce, out loud, what you observe. This will get you out of the past—and future—and focused on the moment . . . that's where intuition waits for you.

All truth passes through three stages: First, it is ridiculed; second, it is violently opposed; and third, it is accepted as self-evident.

— ARTHUR SCHOPENHAUER

*I*n an attempt to fit in, we often become like sheep, meekly following others instead of the power of the Divine Spirit within. Don't allow the fear of standing alone in your truth to turn you into a passive, sheeplike follower. Fit in with angels instead, and be the leader of your life.

*N*ew and stirring things are belittled because if they are not belittled, the humiliating question arises, "Why then are you not taking part in them?"

— H. G. WELLS

The ego becomes threatened when change is introduced, but the Spirit gets excited. The ego rejects what disturbs its control. The Spirit thrills to what promises its freedom.

The word *inspiration* means "to draw from Divine Spirit." Your inspiration will show up by calling your Spirit home, which is accomplished by wanting to hear its voice.

*Intuition becomes increasingly valuable
in the information society precisely
because there is so much data.*

— JOHN NAISBITT

The technological world is
overwhelming if it's not contained.
What do you do when there's so much
information to sift through? How do you
know what is correct for you and what
isn't? Close your eyes, breathe deeply,
relax, go for a long walk, take a soothing
bath, and afford yourself a good night's
sleep. As you rest, ask your Spirit to sort
through all that bombards you and to
supply you with answers when you're
refreshed and able to receive them.

The struggle . . . to learn to
listen to and respect [our] own
intuitive, inner promptings is
the greatest challenge of all.

— HERB GOLDBERG

*Trust your gut. It is *never* wrong.*

— OPRAH WINFREY

*I*ntuition reveals that there is no "them"; there's just "us." It erases the artificial separation from others that our ego-mind creates, reconnecting us to our Universal and eternal Source and our human family. Without it, we're trapped in isolation and fear.

*W*e're reluctant to embrace our inner voice, because with it comes full responsibility for our lives. However, to place that responsibility in the hands of others is a far more frightening thought.

The morning is wiser
than the evening.

— RUSSIAN PROVERB

Tonight before going to bed,
present your concerns and questions
to your Higher Self, the Divine Spirit
within. Ask your Spirit to work
on solutions while you sleep and
to share them with you in the
morning. . . . *Sweet dreams.*

*I*ntuition doesn't necessarily speak on demand. Sometimes you must first quiet your mind and your emotions before it will speak to you. Nothing accomplishes this better than a good night's sleep.

Sixth sense: (noun) grasping the inner nature of things intuitively

— WORDNET 3.0, PRINCETON UNIVERSITY

*W*hen you know, you know.
Let that be enough.

*I*t is one of the commonest of our
mistakes to consider that the limit of
our power of perception is also the
limit of all that there is to perceive.

— C. W. Leadbeater

*N*ever assume that what you
know is all there is to know,
because your Spirit may surprise
you with something more.

*I*f the single man plant himself
indomitably on his instincts, and
there abide, the huge world
will come round to him.

— Ralph Waldo Emerson

There's nothing strange about
intuition, but there is much
that is magical.

[T]here is no instinct like the heart.

— LORD BYRON

*H*ave a conversation with your heart
every day. It has so much to share,
but it prefers to be asked first.

*P*eople only see what
they are prepared to see.

— RALPH WALDO EMERSON

There's nothing that blinds faster or more thoroughly than a closed mind. Open up to your Divine Spirit and everything starts to become clearer.

Intuition is a spiritual faculty and does not explain, but simply points the way.

— FLORENCE SCOVEL SHINN

*S*top talking and listen so that
you can hear your Divine Spirit
whispering in your heart.

*T*he power of intuition
will protect you from harm
until the end of your days.

— LAO-TZU

*T*he Divine Spirit within is a
formidable force, and when honored, it
surrounds you in grace. Your vibration
becomes so high and your focus so
clear that all disturbances and
threats naturally fall away.

*I*t [the theory of relativity] occurred
to me by intuition. And music is the
driving force behind this intuition.
. . . My new discovery is the result
of musical perception.

— ALBERT EINSTEIN

*Y*our Spirit, like your body and mind, needs to be fed in order to stay healthy and alive. Feeding your Spirit strengthens your intuition in every way. Its favorite nourishment is music, poetry, theater, and dance. It also loves art, color, beauty, and movement. Provide your Spirit with these delicacies and it will transform them into creative genius. Have a banquet for the Spirit . . . and reap the rewards!

Sixth sense: (noun) a power of perception like but not one of the five senses: a keen intuitive power

— *MERRIAM-WEBSTER'S COLLEGIATE DICTIONARY*, ELEVENTH EDITION

The sixth sense *is* powerful; and when respected and followed, it will heal your life.

Your inner voice can't be controlled or contained by your intellect. Train your intellect to relax through meditation, and enjoy the creative adventures ahead.

*A*rt arises from the Spirit, and the Spirit speaks through the sixth sense.

[*E*]very time you don't follow your inner guidance you feel a loss of energy, loss of power, a sense of spiritual or emotional deadness.

— SHAKTI GAWAIN

*I*f you lack energy or enthusiasm, it's time to surrender your thoughts and call in your Higher Self, the Divine Spirit within. It's the Source of your vitality; it's the root of your life force. Cooperate with your true Divine nature and you'll feel more fully alive than ever before.

*T*he moment of truth, the sudden emergence of a new insight, is an act of intuition. Such intuitions give the appearance of miraculous flushes, or short-circuits of reasoning. In fact they may be likened to an immersed chain, of which only the beginning and the end are visible above the surface of consciousness. The diver vanishes at one end of the chain and comes up at the other end, guided by invisible links.

— ARTHUR KOESTLER

*I*ntuition makes sense, *perfect sense*
. . . but only from the vantage point
of the Spirit and never from the
perspective of the ego. That's because
the ego prefers control over truth.

*I*f you've lost touch with your
inner voice, find your humor—
it will lead you directly to it.

$\mathcal{C}$old feet are often symptomatic
of a legitimate intuition that you
may be heading for the wrong
place at the wrong time.

— SUZANNE FIELDS

$\mathcal{E}$ven though your ego intellect
can be influenced and persuaded
to go against your deepest truth,
your body cannot.

The more and more each is
impelled by that which is intuitive,
or relying upon the soul force within,
the greater, the farther, the deeper,
the broader, the more constructive
may be the result.

— EDGAR CAYCE

Ignoring your intuition is like driving
on a highway in the dark of night
with your headlights off—on purpose.

*T*urn on the light of your intuition. *Want* to see the way.

*T*he fuel of your intuition is honesty. If you honestly desire answers, you'll get them.

*I*f you want the truth,
I'll tell you the truth:

Listen to the secret sound,
the real sound, which is inside you.

— KABIR

*I*ntuition doesn't tell you
what you *want* to hear; it tells
you what you *need* to hear.

Stop fighting your intuition and give it a chance. It's on your side.

Very often people don't so much doubt their guidance as their ability to follow it. This is where friends—the right kind of friends—come in. Surround yourself with companions who encourage you to trust your inner voice. Keep company with those willing to believe in you. With their help and support, *you* will come to believe in you as well.

*O*ur intuition is our protection.
It watches our back, lights our way,
keeps us out of harm's way, and guides
us toward the discovery and realization
of our highest purpose. It reveals what
the ego can't see—or chooses not to.
It reveals our Divine nature and opens
us up to the secret connection we have
to everything in the Universe.

*T*here is a Secret One inside us;
the planets in all the galaxies
pass through his hands like beads.

That is a string of beads one
should look at with luminous eyes.

— KABIR

All you need to do to receive guidance is to ask for it and then listen.

— Sanaya Roman

Today I affirm that I am Divinely guided. . . . There is That within which knows what to do and how to do it, and It compels me to act on what I know.

— Ernest Holmes

*L*isten to your own Self. If you
listen within, then you find the Truth.

— KABIR

*B*e tenacious—follow your heart
when the whole world screams for
you to get back into your head.

*W*hen you really listen to
yourself, you can heal yourself.

— CEANNE DEROHAN

*S*top the words now. Open the
window in the center of your chest,
and let the spirits fly in and out.

— RUMI

Afterword

As you can see, as children of the Great Creator, we're all gifted with a Divine Presence, known as the *sixth sense,* which can be accessed by simply turning inward and listening to our hearts. It's trustworthy. It's reliable. It's protective and healing—and it won't let us down.

If you doubt *my* word, take the word of the great sages throughout the ages—and throughout these pages—who share my message. Nothing stands between you and your own greatness once you make a personal *decision* to accept your intuition, the voice of the Divine Spirit within, and let it lead you through life. Not only will listening to your sixth sense—your inner voice—guide, nurture, heal, and support your life, it will also make you a healer of others' lives as well.

For each one of us, living in the natural flow of Divine wisdom, in harmony with our true nature as a Divine Being, serve as a role model for others and give them permission, by our example, to embrace their inner wisdom as well. By doing so, we contribute our part to ushering in a new era of greater peace in the world.

So please, for your sake, for our sake—for the *world's* sake—there's no better time than *now* to make the decision to accept and use your intuitive gift, your sixth sense, as you're designed to. And there's no better time than now for you to start enjoying the blessings and grace that will flow from that decision when you do make it.

And from my heart to yours, I send you this final blessing. . . .

May you accept the gift of your sixth sense, the Divine Spirit within. And may this gift empower you in every aspect of your life for the rest of your days, beginning <u>now.</u>

— WITH LOVE, SONIA

About the Author

Sonia Choquette is a world-renowned author, storyteller, vibrational healer, and six-sensory spiritual teacher in international demand for her guidance, wisdom, and capacity to heal the soul. She's the author of several best-selling books, including *Diary of a Psychic, Ask Your Guides,* and *Trust Your Vibes;* and numerous audio programs and card decks. Sonia was educated at the University of Denver and the Sorbonne in Paris, and holds a Ph.D. in metaphysics from the American Institute of Holistic Theology. She resides with her family in Chicago.

Website: **www.soniachoquette.com**

Notes

Notes

Notes

Notes

HAY HOUSE TITLES
OF RELATED INTEREST

YOU CAN HEAL YOUR LIFE, the movie,
starring Louise L. Hay & Friends
(available as a 1-DVD program and
an expanded 2-DVD set)
Watch the trailer at: **www.LouiseHayMovie.com**

HEALING WORDS FROM THE ANGELS:
365 Daily Messages, by Doreen Virtue, Ph.D.

LED BY FAITH:
Learning to Trust God in All Things,
by Immaculée Ilibagiza, with Steve Erwin
(available September 2008)

MANIFEST YOUR DESIRES: 365 Ways to
Make Your Dreams a Reality, by Esther and
Jerry Hicks (The Teachings of Abraham®)

*MESSAGES FROM SPIRIT: The Extraordinary
Power of Oracles, Omens, and Signs,*
by Colette Baron-Reid

*101 WAYS TO JUMP-START YOUR
INTUITION,* by John Holland

*SQUEEZE THE DAY: 365 Ways to Bring JOY
and JUICE into Your Life,* by Loretta LaRoche

*THE PRESENT MOMENT: 365 Daily
Affirmations,* by Louise L. Hay

*YOUR ULTIMATE CALLING: 365 Ways
to Bring Inspiration into Your Life,*
by Dr. Wayne W. Dyer

All of the above are available at your
local bookstore, or may be ordered
by contacting Hay House (see next page).

We hope you enjoyed this Hay House book.
If you'd like to receive a free catalog featuring
additional Hay House books and products,
or if you'd like information about the
Hay Foundation, please contact:

Hay House, Inc.
P.O. Box 5100
Carlsbad, CA 92018-5100

(760) 431-7695 or (800) 654-5126
(760) 431-6948 (fax) or (800) 650-5115 (fax)
www.hayhouse.com® • www.hayfoundation.org

Published and distributed in Australia by:
Hay House Australia Pty. Ltd., 18/36 Ralph St.,
Alexandria NSW 2015 • *Phone:* 612-9669-4299
Fax: 612-9669-4144 • www.hayhouse.com.au

*Published and distributed in the United Kingdom
by:* Hay House UK, Ltd., 292B Kensal Rd.,
London W10 5BE • *Phone:* 44-20-8962-1230
Fax: 44-20-8962-1239 • www.hayhouse.co.uk

Published and distributed in the Republic of South Africa by: Hay House SA (Pty), Ltd., P.O. Box 990, Witkoppen 2068 • *Phone/Fax:* 27-11-467-8904 orders@psdprom.co.za • www.hayhouse.co.za

Published in India by: Hay House Publishers India, Muskaan Complex, Plot No. 3, B-2, Vasant Kunj, New Delhi 110 070 • *Phone:* 91-11-4176-1620 *Fax:* 91-11-4176-1630 • www.hayhouse.co.in

Distributed in Canada by: Raincoast, 9050 Shaughnessy St., Vancouver, B.C. V6P 6E5 *Phone:* (604) 323-7100 • *Fax:* (604) 323-2600 www.raincoast.com

Tune in to **HayHouseRadio.com**® for the best in inspirational talk radio featuring top Hay House authors! And, sign up via the Hay House USA Website to receive the Hay House online newsletter and stay informed about what's going on with your favorite authors. You'll receive bimonthly announcements about Discounts and Offers, Special Events, Product Highlights, Free Excerpts, Giveaways, and more!
www.hayhouse.com®

BE HEALED
IN JESUS' NAME

BY

JOYCE MEYER

Harrison House
Tulsa, Oklahoma

Be Healed in Jesus' Name
ISBN 1-57794-173-X
Copyright © 2000 by Joyce Meyer
Life In The Word, Inc.
P. O. Box 655
Fenton, Missouri 63026

06 05 04 03 02   18 17 16 15 14 13 12 11 10 9 8 7 6 5 4

Published by Harrison House, Inc.
P. O. Box 35035
Tulsa, Oklahoma 74153

CONTENTS

1
RELEASING GOD'S
POWER TO HEAL

Many people believe God is **able** to heal them but aren't sure whether He **will** heal them. If you are one of those people, in this book you will find Scripture verses that reveal how willing God is to heal. You will also find an explanation of how to receive the healing God has for you according to the principles He gave us in the Bible.

Those principles may surprise you! They do **not** involve making yourself good enough to receive healing. God is a

loving Father Who wants to do good
things for His children. He wants to
make us well.

If your child became sick and you had
the ability to heal that child, you would
do it. God is a much better parent than
any of us could ever be. He wants to heal
His children, and He has the ability to do
it. He wants to do anything for us that
will make our lives better.

Jesus said:

> *The thief* (referring to Satan) *comes only in
> order to steal and kill and destroy. I came that
> they may have and enjoy life, and have it in
> abundance (to the full, till it overflows).*
>
> *John 10:10*

First John 3:8 (KJV) tells us:

...For this purpose the Son of God was manifested, that he might destroy the works of the devil.

Jesus came to earth to destroy the works of the devil so that we *might have life, and have it more abundantly* (John 10:10 KJV).

Psalm 103 describes the benefits the loving Father has for His children. Verse 3 tells us one of those benefits is healing.

Bless (affectionately, gratefully praise) the Lord, O my soul, and forget not [one of] all His benefits —
Who forgives [every one of] all your iniquities,
Who heals [each one of] all your diseases,
Who redeems your life from the pit and corruption, Who beautifies, dignifies, and crowns you with loving-kindness and tender mercy;
Who satisfies your mouth [your necessity and desire at your personal age and situation]

with good so that your youth, renewed, is like
the eagle's [strong, overcoming, soaring]!
Verses 2-5

Proverbs 4:20-22, one of the Scripture passages that reveals God's willingness to heal us, also contains one of the principles God gives us in His Word for receiving healing.

*My son, **attend to my words;** incline thine ear*
unto my sayings.
Let them not depart from thine eyes; keep
them in the midst of thine heart.

*For **they are life** unto those that find them,*
*and **health to all their flesh** (KJV).*

In Proverbs 4:20-22 Solomon is speaking of **God's** words, which we find in the Bible, "His Word." His words *unto those that find them* are *life* and *health to* *all their flesh!* (v. 22). *The Amplified Bible* includes the word "healing" in verse 22: *healing and health to all their flesh.*

According to *Strong's Exhaustive Concordance of the Bible* the Hebrew word translated "health" in verse 22 also means "a medicine."[1]

Exodus 15:26 says, ...*I am the LORD that healeth thee* (KJV). Isaac Leesser translates this verse: ...*I the Lord am thy physician.*[2] Psalm 107:20 (KJV) tells us: *He* (the Lord) *sent his word, and healed them, and delivered them from their destructions.*

The Lord is our Physician; the medicine He prescribes is His Word.

Because God's words are healing, or medicine, to those who find them, then a biblical principle to follow in order to receive healing is *attend* to God's *words!*

When you attend to something, you pay close attention to it. Learning the information in God's Word about His ability and willingness to heal and the methods He uses is similar to learning all you can about a doctor you are seeing for the first time.

You want to know that the doctor is qualified, experienced and capable of evaluating your health condition and prescribing the best treatment. The information you learn about the doctor gives you confidence to receive the advice and recommended treatment as the best approach for bringing the healing you need.

In the same way, to build confidence in God's willingness and ability to treat your condition, you learn about Him by reading His Word. When you attend to God's words on healing, you learn that God wants to do more than treat your condition — He wants to heal you completely!

We receive from God through faith. Mark 9:23 (NASB) tells us, ...*All things are possible to him who believes.*

> *So then faith comes by hearing, and hearing by the word of God.*
>
> Romans 10:17 NKJV

Hearing God's Word on healing is important so that faith to receive the healing God has for you will come. But attending to God's words on healing is very important for another reason. The power to heal is actually inherent **in** God's Word. **It is the Word itself that heals you.**

*God's Words Contain
the Power to Heal*

God's words, life unto those that find them (KJV) and healing and health to all their flesh (as we saw in Proverbs 4:22), are sharp and powerful! Hebrews 4:12 (KJV) tells us: *For the word of God is quick, and powerful, and sharper than any twoedged sword....*

Jesus said, *...the words that I speak unto you, they are spirit, and they are life* (John 6:63 KJV). Jesus' words, recorded in the Bible, are Spirit and life. God's Word contains energy and ability!

Proverbs 18:21 tells us, *Death and life are in the power of the tongue....* God's Word is a container for His power. When we activate His power by speaking His Word, His Word spoken out our mouth contains power. Our words containing His power become like little bullets of *life* and *health* that shoot out into *all* our *flesh* to change our lives.

When I am teaching and speaking God's Word, it's as though I can see power in the words coming out my mouth, carrying God's healing ability to the people in the congregation.

When that power begins to hit the people listening, they can bathe in it. They can be cleansed *by the washing of water with the Word* (Ephesians 5:26).

And God's Word accomplishes what it is sent out to do.

*Releasing God's Healing
Through Speaking His Words*

*So shall My word be that goes forth out of My
mouth: it shall not return to Me void [without
producing any effect, useless], but it shall
accomplish that which I please and purpose,
and it shall prosper in the thing for which I
sent it.*

Isaiah 55:11

To learn the benefits God has made available to us, we attend to His Word by reading or hearing it. To bring into physical evidence the benefits we have learned are ours from His Word, we speak the Word in faith. And according to Isaiah 55:11 God's spoken Word does not return to Him void without prospering in the thing for which it was sent.

We release God's power to heal by speaking His Word with confidence in His ability and willingness to heal our condition.

2

GOD WANTS GOOD THINGS FOR HIS CHILDREN

In order to have faith for something in any area, we must know it is God's will for the particular thing we are praying for to happen. We won't be able to use our faith to receive healing if we are not sure it is God's will.

In this section we look at the scriptural basis for believing that God wants each one of us to receive healing. It is important for us to understand that God as a

Parent wants good things for His children. Matthew 7:11 (KJV) says:

> If ye then, being evil, know how to give good gifts unto your children, **how much more shall your Father which is in heaven give good things to them that ask him?**

God wants to do good things for us because He loves us. We can **begin** to understand how much the Father loves us if we think about how much we love our children. However, God loves us because He **is** love. Love is not something He does; love is Who He is. (1 John 4:16.)

Love is all God knows how to do. And the Bible says, ...*God is no respecter of persons* (Acts 10:34 KJV). He does not love one person more than He loves another one. He does not love the preacher at church more than He loves you, or the man working in the sound booth, or the piano player or the most prominent person you can think of. But sometimes we think that way — we think God loves other people more than He loves us!

God's love for us is complete, pure, steady, constant and unending. We can't be separated from it. (See Romans 8:38,39.)

God wants to have a personal relationship with us because, as a loving Father, there is so much He wants to do for us. He wants us to receive all the benefits He has for us that we read about in Psalm 103. To provide a Way for us to have a personal relationship with Him, God sent His Son, Jesus. Jesus said, ..."*I am the way, and the truth, and the life; no one* comes to the Father, but through Me" (John 14:6 NASB).

We receive everything the Father has for us through Jesus: not only salvation — eternal life with the Father — but the benefits described in Psalm 103:2-5 and everything else.

> In this was manifested **the love of God** toward us, because that **God sent his only begotten Son** into the world, **that we might live through him.**
>
> *1 John 4:9 KJV*

> For **God so loved the world, that he gave his only begotten Son,** that **whosoever believeth in him** should not perish, **but have everlasting life.**
>
> *John 3:16 KJV*

The Scripture below shows us how much the Father wants to *freely give us all things.*

> He that spared not his own Son, but delivered him up for us all, how shall he not with him also freely give us all things?
>
> *Romans 8:32 KJV*

The problem is not on God's side — He is not withholding good things from us. The problem is on our side — not being able to receive what He has already made freely available for us. Many of us don't freely receive many, or any, of *all things* the Father has for us because we don't know they are available. Others of us who know what good things He has for us, don't know how to receive them.

First, to become an heir of God, of *all things* He has for us, we establish a personal relationship with Him by believing in His Son, Jesus. Galatians 3:26 (KJV) tells us: *For ye are all the children of God by faith in Christ Jesus.* And as a son (or child) of God, we become an heir of God, a fellow heir with Jesus. (See Romans 8:17, Galatians 4:7.)*

Also, to receive all the Father has for us, we must fully consider the great price Jesus paid for the purpose of making eternal life and all the other benefits freely available to us.

---

* If you do not have a personal relationship with God, see the prayer at the end of this book to learn how to allow Him to come into your life.

We saw in John 3:16 that whoever believes in God's Son will *have everlasting life.* And God wants all men to be saved — to receive everlasting, eternal life with Him.

Sozo:
Saved, to Be Made Whole

The Greek word **sozo** is translated in some Scripture passages as "saved." **Sozo** is also translated in other passages as "...'to make whole,' and, in the passive voice, 'to be made whole,' or 'to be whole....'"[1]

In the two Scripture verses below, **sozo,** translated as "saved," describes receiving salvation through the Mediator between God and man, Jesus.

*For this is good and acceptable in the sight of
God our Saviour;*

*Who will have all men to be **saved,** and to
come unto the knowledge of the truth.*

*For there is one God, and one mediator
between God and men, the man Christ Jesus.*

1 Timothy 2:3-5 KJV

*That if thou shalt confess with thy mouth the
Lord Jesus, and shalt believe in thine heart
that God hath raised him from the dead, thou
shalt be **saved.***

*For with the heart man believeth unto
righteousness; and with the mouth confession
is made unto salvation.*

Romans 10:9,10 KJV

The same Greek word **sozo** is translated
"whole" (as in deliverance "from sickness") — *"made...whole"* — in Matthew
9:22[2] (KJV) below.

*But Jesus turned him about, and when he saw her, he said, Daughter, be of good comfort; thy faith hath made thee **whole**. And the woman was made whole from that hour.*

Jesus came not only to save us, but to make us whole in every way — to heal us. Do you see from the Scriptures we have looked at to this point how much God wants you to receive healing? He wants you to be completely made whole in **every** area of your life.

3
THE BASIS FOR RECEIVING HEALING

Jesus said:

The Spirit of the Lord is upon me, because he
hath anointed me to preach the gospel to the
poor; he hath sent me to heal the
brokenhearted, to preach deliverance to the
captives, and recovering of sight to the blind,
to set at liberty them that are bruised.

Luke 4:18 KJV

Jesus continually healed people in His
earthly ministry. In Matthew chapters 8
and 9, we read of Jesus healing person
after person.

If you ever want to become encouraged concerning your healing, just open your Bible to Matthew chapters 8 and 9 and start reading. These two chapters contain one account after another of Jesus healing people who had diseases.

In this book we are establishing that it is God's will for people to be healed physically. There are many accounts in God's Word of the tremendous healings Jesus did, even bringing people back from the dead. Jesus also affirmed over and over that He came only to do the Father's will. (See John 6:38; John 5:19).

From the many accounts in the Bible of Jesus healing people and His statements that He came only to do the Father's

will, we can see that it **is** God's will for
people to be physically healed.

Healing Is God's Will

Hebrews 13:8 (KJV) tells us *Jesus Christ
is the same yesterday, and to day, and for
ever.* We can't say that healing passed
away with the early church, which some
people teach. What Jesus did in the days
He was walking on the earth, He will
also do for you today. If He was healing
people then, He is certainly about the
business of healing people today.

Isaiah 53 contains some of the most
powerful teaching in God's Word on the
subject of healing. *The Amplified Bible*
makes the meaning of this passage
crystal clear.

Verses 4 and 5 state:

Surely He has borne our griefs (sicknesses, weaknesses, and distresses) and carried our sorrows and pains [of punishment], yet we [ignorantly] considered Him stricken, smitten, and afflicted by God [as if with leprosy].

But He was wounded for our transgressions, He was bruised for our guilt and iniquities; the chastisement [needful to obtain] peace and well-being for us was upon Him, and with the stripes [that wounded] Him we are healed and made whole.

The word, "surely," that begins verse 4, doesn't leave any room for doubt.[1] *Surely He has borne our* ("our" means yours and my) *griefs (sicknesses, weaknesses, and distresses) and carried our sorrows and pains [of punishment]....* The *New International Version* of the Bible words this portion of the verse, *Surely he took up our infirmities and carried our sorrows....*

Verse 4 (AMP) continues:

> *...yet we* [ignorantly] *considered Him stricken, smitten, and afflicted by God....*

One day as I was praying, God began to unfold to me a revelation about Isaiah 53:4,5. As I began to realize how many times we ignorantly consider Jesus — how many times we ignorantly consider what He **died** for us to have — I just began to weep.

Instead of seeing God as the Father Who loves us so much and wants to do so many things for us, many of us see Him through the eyes of religion. And "religion" does not always represent the good God the Scriptures reveal Him to be, the God I know, at all.

Jesus died, not because He was stricken and afflicted by God for something He did, but to take our sicknesses and diseases on His body so that we wouldn't have to experience those things.

Again Isaiah 53:5 (AMP) says:

> ...the chastisement [needful to obtain] peace and well-being for us was upon Him, and with the stripes [that wounded] Him we are healed and made whole.

Jesus died to bring us salvation, peace and healing.

As you read this, close your eyes for a moment after each description, and use your imagination. (God created your imagination to be holy and used for godly purposes.)

Before Jesus went to Calvary to be crucified on the cross, He was probably tied to some kind of a post, we believe, as was done before a Roman execution.[2]

In your imagination see Jesus tied to the post, and see a soldier, who is probably rather large, come out with a whip that has several strips of leather with little pieces of sharp bone and metal tied into each piece of leather.[3] See Jesus begin to receive those stripes that He took for the healing that you need.

One, two, three, four — He is probably starting to bleed, now — five, six, seven — I'm sure He's writhing in pain. Eight, nine, ten... The Romans didn't necessarily limit the number of stripes to the thirty-nine of Jewish law.[4] Jesus bore our sicknesses and diseases, taking them upon His own body, to the point, the Bible teaches, that He became totally unrecognizable. He wasn't even recognizable as a man. (See Isaiah 52:14 NIV.)

Jesus underwent that terrible persecution, humiliation and grueling beating, to the point of being unrecognizable as a man, then an excruciating, horrible death to take on our sin **and** to bear our sicknesses and diseases. He died not only for us to receive salvation — everlasting life with God through believing in Jesus — **but also** to provide healing for us.

The New Testament Scriptures below describe Jesus as fulfilling the prophecy of Isaiah 53 to provide **both** salvation and healing.

First Corinthians 15:3 tells us: ...*Christ (the Messiah, the Anointed One) died for our sins in accordance with [what] the Scriptures [foretold]* (referring to Isaiah 53:5-12).[5] Jesus died to take on our sins so ...*that whoever believes in him shall not perish but have eternal life* (John 3:16 NIV).

Matthew 8:16 states:

When evening came, they brought to Him (Jesus) many who were under the power of demons, and He drove out the spirits with a word and restored to health all who were sick.

Verse 17, after describing the healings Jesus performed in verse 16, tells us:

And thus He fulfilled what was spoken by the prophet Isaiah. He Himself took [in order to

*carry away] our weaknesses and infirmities
and bore away our diseases.*

First Peter 2:24 (KJV) states that we were
healed by Jesus' stripes.

*Who his own self bare our sins in his own
body on the tree, that we, being dead to sins,
should live unto righteousness: by whose
stripes ye were healed.*

Jesus bore the stripes that were needful
to obtain your healing. When you let a
revelation of what Jesus did for you
unfold to you, rather than concentrating
on trying to figure out the answers to
your problem, I believe that sickness and
disease will not be able to remain attached
to your body.

Fully consider the great price Jesus paid
so that God could *freely give us all things,*

and take hold of **all** the benefits available to you as a child and an heir of God.

God wants you to receive the healing you need. Take hold of your healing by faith.

4
SIMPLE FAITH

We receive healing in the same way we receive everything else from God: through faith. Paul's description of the Colossians' faith in Christ in *The Amplified Bible* is the best definition of faith I've ever heard: *...[that leaning of the entire human personality on Him* (described as God in Christ in Hebrews 6:12) *in absolute trust and confidence in His power, wisdom, and goodness]* (Colossians 2:5).

Faith Is Leaning on God

Having faith is not complicated. From Paul's definition we can see that faith is simply leaning on God in trust and confidence.

There is a little animal called a limpet that we can learn to be like in a way when it comes to leaning on God in simple faith. The limpet, a marine animal with a shell and a muscular foot, does one thing extremely well — it clings tightly to rocks.[1]

If you were walking along the seashore and approached a limpet on a rock without it sensing you were there, you could strike it with your walking stick, and it would fall.

A second limpet, further down on the same rock, sensing the danger would immediately react with its tremendous ability to cling. If you struck it, you wouldn't be able to knock it off the rock no matter how hard you tried, once it had begun to cling. That limpet wouldn't understand exactly what was happening — it wouldn't understand you, your walking stick or the intricate details of how God created its anatomy to work with the rock formation for the limpet's protection — it would simply do the one thing it knew how to do — cling!

In a similar way, you may not understand everything you would like to know about the doctrine of faith or exactly how God's words can be health or medicine to your flesh. But understanding those things is not a requirement for you to receive healing, or any of the other benefits, from God. God's requirement for you is simply this: Cling in faith to Jesus.

Use the Faith You Have

Sometimes people who want a healing more than anything are not sure they have enough faith to receive it. I want to encourage you that (as we saw before) Romans 10:17 tells us when we hear the Word of God, faith comes. If you have a personal relationship with God by believing in Jesus, God is in you through the power of the Holy Spirit. And where God is, there is faith. Romans 12:3 (KJV) tells us, ...*God hath dealt to every man the measure of faith.* If God is in you, you already have faith!

When you hear the Word of God spoken and faith **comes,** I believe the *measure of faith* inside you rises up to meet the Word, and together they **go** out to do the job. Remember, it is the Word that heals you. When you speak God's words, they will *accomplish* and *prosper in the thing* they were sent to do (as we saw in Isaiah 55:11).

We see in the Scripture below that faith the size of a grain of a mustard seed is enough to move a mountain! When Jesus' disciples asked Him why they were unable to cast out a demon:

He [Jesus] said to them, Because of the littleness of your faith [that is, your lack of firmly relying trust]. For truly I say to you, if you have faith [that is living] like a grain of mustard seed, you can say to this mountain,

Move from here to yonder place, and it will
move; and nothing will be impossible to you.
Matthew 17:20

People who are concerned that they
don't have enough faith for healing need
instead to turn their attention to learning
how to use the faith they already have.
Don't be concerned about whether your
faith is perfect — release what you have
and watch God work in your behalf.

Receive Healing As a Gift

Sometimes people want healing so
badly that, without realizing it, they
actually start **working** to try to **earn** it
from God. They **try** to get enough faith
to be healed instead of receiving healing

from Him as one of the things He freely wants to give us.

You can't **earn** healing with great faith or anything else. You can't **buy** healing with your faith. Healing is not for sale. It has already been bought with the blood of Jesus. You can only **receive** healing with your faith. Faith is an avenue for receiving, not legal tender or money to use in buying something. There is a difference. Faith is a **gift** that is given to you, and you must receive it as a gift.

Romans 12:3 (KJV) tells us, ...*God hath dealt to every man the measure of faith.* The *New International Version* words this verse as ...*the measure of faith God has given you.*

I can well remember feeling condemned because I thought I did not have strong enough faith. If I prayed and did not get well right away, I began to receive Satan's lie that "I did not have enough faith."

One day I finally became tired of feeling condemned, and I said out loud as a declaration — "I have the amount of faith I have, and I'm going to keep using what I have instead of worrying about what I don't have."

Believing is actually an act of the will, a decision, based upon what we have learned to be true about God. It is leaning on Him *in absolute trust and confidence* based upon our knowledge of how good He is and that He will do what He says in His Word.

We can **decide** to believe, then rest in the knowledge that the Word will *accomplish* and *prosper in the thing* it was sent to do. Real faith is a rest, not a struggle. Those who believe enter into the rest of God. (Hebrews 4:3.) It is wonderful to be in God's rest while we are waiting for the full manifestation of our healing.

Like the little limpet, cling to the rock. Cling to the Rock (1 Corinthians 10:4), Jesus, confidently waiting to receive what is rightfully yours as an heir of God through the blood Jesus shed to make it available for you.

Even now as I write this book, my husband, Dave, is waiting to see the manifestation of a physical healing that he needs and we are believing God for. He developed a blood clot in his leg and has been lying around for twelve days with his leg propped up. He is taking his medicine as the doctor recommended, but he is also taking the medicine of God's Word while steadfastly believing that God will completely remove the problem and that it will never return. Medicine usually treats symptoms; God's power removes the problem.

Dave is not frustrated or upset; he is in the rest of God because he is believing. He is not feeling condemned because he has not seen the full result yet. He is being thankful for each stage of progress, and he knows that ...*God causes all things to work together for good to those who love*

God, to those who are called according to His purpose (Romans 8:28 NASB).

Probably by the time you read this book, Dave will be completely well, but right now he is waiting just as you and many other people reading this book may be. We inherit the promises of God through faith and patience. (Hebrews 10:36.) There are times when we receive instant results from our prayers and other times when we must wait and be patient. It is not our responsibility to reason out "why and when"; we are to simply remain in childlike faith, knowing that our loving heavenly Father will always take good care of us and that it is impossible for Him to fail.

5

HINDRANCES TO HEALING

Our relationship with our heavenly Father is one of love. (See 1 John 4:16 KJV.) To receive from God, you must receive His love. You must believe that He loves you. And because He first loved us, we love Him back. (1 John 4:19.) Our loving Parent/child relationship with Him is similar to a loving parent/child relationship on earth. We relate to our heavenly Father by doing things pleasing to Him because we love Him.

He wants what is best for us. He wants us to walk in the Spirit — to live in a state of being open to Him, able to hear His voice — so that we will receive all he has for us in every area of life.

If we are intentionally living a life full of sin without any desire or attempt to stop, if we aren't seeking God to help us change, we are walking in the flesh. Just as a loving earthly parent will not give privileges to a child who is purposely belligerent, rebellious and disobedient, God will not give us privileges that will encourage us to walk in the flesh.

This does not mean that you must be doing everything perfectly for God to heal you. None of us is perfect in our performance. We can have a perfect heart toward God, a really sincere desire to do all things according to His will. According to Matthew 5:48 in *The Amplified Bible,* we grow into that perfection. The presence of the Holy Spirit inside of us makes us perfect in heart, but it takes some time for the flesh to get in line with the heart. We may make mistakes and do some things wrong, but God judges according to the heart. Understanding this will help you enter God's rest and receive all the good things He has for you.

Having something wrong in your life does not mean God will not heal you. But receiving *everything* God has for you — abundance in finances, divine health and in other areas of life — is based

upon your relationship with your Father.
Your heart must be right toward Him to
receive from Him.

God wants your will to be in line with
His will. He wants your thoughts to be in
line with His thoughts as revealed in His
Word. He wants your emotions to be
under the control of the Holy Spirit.

Third John 2 tells us:

> Beloved, I pray that you may prosper in every
> way and [that your body] may keep well, even
> as [I know] your soul keeps well and prospers.

If God is showing you something in your
life that needs to be moved out of the way,
He is not showing it to you to condemn
you. He wants you to see how to operate
differently in order to line up with His will

so that you will be able to easily receive everything He has to give you.

God wants your soul — your mind, will and emotions — to prosper. Most of the time your physical man will not prosper beyond the level that your soulish man has prospered. God wants to be the Lord of the soulish realm as well as the spiritual and physical realm.

If you are full of bitterness, resentment and unforgiveness or have all kinds of open, known sin in your life and don't even care, in all probability you will not receive the physical healing you desire. But even though it is unlikely, God sometimes does perform a miracle, a healing, in a situation like this. Occasionally God will show Himself strong in someone's life in this way to demonstrate His love, to draw the person's attention to Him.

God wants to heal you, but He expects you to bring your soulish man in line with His Word. Spiritual maturity should be our #1 goal. It is even more important than our physical healing.

One of the greatest ways to clog up your pipe of faith, so to speak, is to have unforgiveness in your heart. You won't be able to receive very much from God if you are harboring unforgiveness, bitterness and resentment against someone else. The Bible clearly tells us that if we will not forgive other people of their sins, God will not forgive us. (See Mark 11:25,26 NASB.)

Matthew 9:2 gives an account of Jesus healing a paralytic, brought on a bed to Him. The first thing Jesus said to the paralytic was, ...*your sins are forgiven you* (Matthew 9:2 NKJV). In this instance when the person was brought to Jesus for healing, He forgave the person's sins, and the paralytic was healed. (vv. 6,7.)

James 5:16 relates that we should confess our faults to be healed.

Confess to one another therefore your faults (your slips, your false steps, your offenses, your sins) and pray [also] for one another, that you may be healed and restored [to a spiritual tone of mind and heart]....

The Scriptures show us how important it is to forgive. It would be a good idea to take a few steps back to make sure you aren't holding anything against anyone else, including anything that you may be angry at God about!

It is important that we keep sin out of our life, and God has provided the Way for us to keep our sins covered under the blood of Jesus through true, heartfelt repentance. (See Matthew 26:28.)

If you have sin in your life and you know it, you need to deal with it. Repent. Confess the sin. First John 1:9 (KJV) tells us: *If we confess our sins, he is faithful and just to forgive us our sins, and to cleanse us from all unrighteousness.*

Many people make sin much harder to deal with than it actually is by continuing to dwell on the sin after they repented and asked for forgiveness.

Sometimes people who know that God can heal them are not really sure He will. They look at themselves and think, *Am I too bad for God to heal?* Or they think they aren't as close to God or as "holy" as they think they need to be.

God understands where each of us is spiritually and emotionally, and He will meet us where we are if we will trust Him. Repent; accept forgiveness; turn from the sin and go on! God is faithful and just to forgive you and cleanse you from all unrighteousness. Then cling to Jesus in faith!

Unconfessed personal sin can be the root cause of sickness and disease, but that is not always the case. We live in a sinful world that is filled with germs and forces that break down our immune systems. Don't be too introspective, always trying to figure out what your sin is that caused you to have problems. Be open to God, do some soul searching, but don't go on a digging expedition that causes you to focus on yourself and everything that is wrong with you instead of focusing on Jesus and all that He is able to do for you.

As I have said before, if you have sinned, confess it, receive forgiveness and go on. If God shows you nothing in particular, then don't start imagining things. Stay in God's rest and hold fast your confession of faith in Him. I have discovered in my years of experience with God that He is well able to let me know loud and clear when I have displeased Him. I don't have to guess and get into reasoning to try to figure out why — I know!

There are times when other people can make us feel guilty and as if we must have done something wrong or we would not be having the problems we are having. I can remember one time in particular when one of our children got into some pretty serious trouble. The questions that friends were asking Dave and me definitely indicated that they were searching for what Dave and I had not done right as parents that caused the child to behave this way.

One of his teachers even asked him if he thought he got into trouble because

Dave and I traveled in ministry and were not home with him all the time. They wanted to know if he felt loved and cared for. He promptly told them that He loved us very much and we loved him very much and that he got into trouble because he made wrong choices, not because we traveled.

Obviously, if we had not been maintaining a right relationship with him, that could have been the root of his problem, but my point is that people often jump to conclusions and say things that can make us feel guilty and condemned. It is always best to listen to God and not necessarily to people when it comes to finding out what the root cause of your problem is. The truth was, we had worked very hard in our life to make sure we kept right relationship with our children and that they knew they were very important to us.

There have been times when I was sick and people actually said to me, "You must have sin in your life or this would not be happening," and, "Something must be wrong or you would be receiving your healing!" These same people had a totally different attitude later in life when they became sick and did not find answers to their situation immediately. It is very easy to judge people and say hurtful things when we have not experienced what they are going through. I always find mercy to be more powerful than judgment.

Misconceptions
That Prevent Healing

Many religious doctrines, traditions of thinking contrary to the truth of God's Word, and misconceptions are taught that have kept people from receiving healing from God. We saw that without an understanding of the cleansing power of God's forgiveness, some people think they are too bad for God to heal.

Others have been taught that God gives us sickness in order to teach us something. Stopping to consider what it actually means for God to be our loving Parent, as we have done in this book, will help people realize that teaching isn't true.

For example, no loving parent would teach a two- or three-year-old baby not to play with fire on the stove by putting the child's hand in the fire! In the same way God does not teach us things by making us sick. Yes, God corrects us, but He does it as our loving Parent. (Proverbs 3:12.)

God knows how to correct me when I get out of line and need to be corrected, and He also knows how to correct you. He doesn't have to do it by whipping up a little cancer or a little arthritis or a car wreck to throw on us!

If you are a parent, how do you treat and teach your children whom you love so much? To teach your children to look for cars before crossing a street, would you put your children in the middle of the road then have a car run over them?

You wouldn't do anything like that to teach your children something! And God, your loving Father, won't do anything like that to you to teach you something, either!

Hebrews 12:9 states that God is *the Father of spirits.* He deals with us on a spiritual level. God is the Father of my spirit, and you probably feel the same way I do if you've ever been "spanked" in the spirit by God — I would rather be sick in my flesh any day of the week than to be "sick" in my spirit.

If it is true that God puts sickness on you to teach you something, or that it is God's will for you to be sick on occasion, then you would be out of God's will by taking an aspirin, going to the doctor or doing anything else to recover from a sickness. You would be out of God's will to attend any meeting that had prayer for the sick because you might receive a healing when it was God's will for you to be sick.

If it is God's will for you to be sick so that He can teach you something, the best thing you can do if you are sick is lie down and get as sick as possible!

When you look at this tradition of teaching in this way, the teaching doesn't make sense! But there are literally thousands of Christians who are held captive in that area because they have been taught that sickness is God's will. That teaching has convinced them that we can glorify God by suffering and being patient in sickness. If that doctrine is true, then Jesus robbed God of a great deal of glory when He healed so many sick people who were suffering!

Tradition says the age of miracles has passed away. Once when I was preparing to teach, God impressed something upon me as I was praying. He said, "Tell them not only has the age of miracles not passed away, but I have not even begun yet."

God is going forward, not backward! If the early church needed the miracle-working power of God, how much more do we need it today? Some of the traditions people are taught and the beliefs they hold as a result are foolish. But often those people have believed the teaching for so long, they have never thought to carefully examine the doctrines to determine if they are true!

Tradition says that it is God's will to heal some people, but not all. If that were true, how could you have faith to be healed if you had to first find out if you were one of the favored ones whom God had selected to heal?

...God is no respecter of persons (Acts 10:34 KJV). His will is healing and wholeness. His timing and methods may be different in every case, but His will remains the same. Knowing this is the major key to trusting God all the way through and continuing to stand on His Word.

Joy and peace are found in believing. (Romans 15:13 KJV.) Doubt and unbelief only make us more miserable. When Abraham had no human reason to hope, he hoped on in faith. (Romans 4:18.) We can rejoice in our hope; we can believe for change. All the while we stay positive that the power of God's Word is working in our bodies, bringing them to a place of strength and health.

Job's Afflictions
and Paul's Thorn

People often ask questions about two accounts given in the Bible concerning healing: "Why was Job afflicted?" and "Why did the apostle Paul suffer with a thorn in the flesh?"

Job 1:1 – 2:8 gives the account of the series of sudden, devastating tragedies, including an affliction of boils which covered his entire body, that overcame Job, a godly man of great wealth.

Setting Your Standard

Job 1:4,5 gives us insight that Job often operated out of fear rather than faith. Job's sons held feasts in honor of each other's birthdays. After the period of feasting was completed, Job sent for his sons and had them purified. He also offered burnt offerings early in the morning to God for each son. Job was afraid that his sons might have sinned.

Concerning other circumstances, Job stated: *For the thing which I greatly fear comes upon me, and that of which I am afraid befalls me* (Job 3:25).

Job had a powerful relationship with God and knew better than to operate in fear. But Job was operating in fear instead of faith, and that fear opened the door for Satan to attack him.

God gives us principles to operate within for our own good and protection. When we operate outside of those principles, we are moving into an area that has opened a door for Satan to enter. And in that area, there may be little God can do to protect us at the time.

The Lord later ...*turned the captivity of Job and restored his fortunes...* and ...*gave Job twice as much as he had before* (Job 42:10). But the losses and afflictions Job experienced before then were so devastating

that Job wished he had never been born.
(Job 3:3.)

Second Corinthians 12:7 refers to Paul's
thorn in the flesh which Paul describes as
the messenger of Satan to buffet me.

> And lest I should be exalted above measure
> through the abundance of the revelations,
> there was given to me a thorn in the flesh, the
> messenger of Satan to buffet me, lest I should
> be exalted above measure (KJV).

Much has been written about the
identity of Paul's thorn.

"The thorn was designated as a
'messenger of Satan,' perhaps to indicate
that Satan, as an adversary, resisted
Paul's ministry....the thorn may refer to
some physical infirmity...." or "...to some
painful experience which was spiritual in

nature, such as temptation or the opposition of the Jews."[1]

It may have been "...some great trouble or some great temptation...." or "...the indignities done him by the false apostles, and the opposition he met with from them...."[2]

No matter what Paul's thorn was, when it comes to healing, the identity of Paul's thorn doesn't really matter. The answer to the questions "Why was Job afflicted?" and "Why did the apostle Paul suffer with a thorn in the flesh?" is simply this: Neither Paul nor Job is your standard.

Jesus Is Your Standard

Let us believe we can have what Jesus had, not what Paul or Job had. Jesus walked in divine health, and that should be our goal.

If you feel that you can never reach a level higher than one Job, Paul or other great people of faith reached, you are looking at people as your standard instead of Jesus. You are interpreting Romans 8:17 to read:

> *And if we are [His] children, then we are [His] heirs also: heirs of God and fellow heirs [or joint-heirs KJV] with... **Job**... or ...with **Paul**...!*

The standard God gave us is this: *fellow heirs* [or *joint-heirs* KJV] *with Christ!*

Joint-Heirs with Jesus

Everything that belongs to the Father belongs to Jesus. (John 17:10 NASB.)

Hebrews 1:2 tells us that God appointed His Son *Heir and lawful Owner of all* things.

Everything God has for you, He gives to you because you are a joint-heir with Jesus Christ. You have a right to everything Jesus has!

By believing that you can have everything Jesus has, you are looking at the standard God wants for you. *We must keep fixing our eyes on Jesus, the author and perfecter of faith...* (Hebrews 12:2 NASB).

Many times we have a tendency to look at ourselves or circumstances instead of looking at God. We need to keep fixing our eyes on Jesus and looking at what God said He can and will do.

*Why Don't Some People
Receive Healing?*

If a healing that was desired and prayed
for does not happen, we may or may not
ever learn the reason. The Bible says *our
knowledge is fragmentary* — we know *in
part* (1 Corinthians 13:9,12.)

We don't know everything there is to
know. But instead of focusing on what
we don't know by trying to find a reason
that, in many cases, can't be determined,
we need to focus and build our faith on
the truth we *do* know: what the Bible
teaches about healing.

We don't have all the answers, but we
can reach the point of realizing we don't
have to know them all, as long as we
know the One Who does. There is a

tremendous rest that comes with realizing that we don't have to understand
everything that happens.

I used to allow myself to become
confused if someone I knew who was
believing God for healing did not receive
it. Sometimes the person was me, and
other times it was someone else. I finally
learned through years of experience that
I needed to trust God even in things I
could not mentally understand.

I have prayed many times and received
healing, but at other times I had to walk
through a sickness. Sometimes I have
received healing quickly, and other times
I have had to wait much longer than I
would have liked to. I have seen people
who were absolute skeptics concerning

the doctrine of supernatural healing receive great miracles, and yet others who seemed to have all the faith in the world have remained sick or even died.

I don't have all those answers, but I made up my mind that according to God's Word physical healing is part of our inheritance, and I am going to keep believing and stay away from reasoning *...that sets itself up against the [true] knowledge of God...*(2 Corinthians 10:5). I may need to go to the doctor, but I am still believing God. I may have to wait and go through some things, but I am still going to believe God's Word and stand in faith that I will have a complete victory in God's timing, however He chooses to minister to me.

Don't allow yourself to become confused; just keep believing. Jesus told Mary and Martha in John 11:40 that if they would keep on believing, they would see the glory of God. Often we must "keep on believing" for a while before we see a breakthrough.

God Is Working for Us

And so faith, hope, love abide....
1 Corinthians 13:13

It is a tremendous comfort to know that even though we don't always understand why some things happen, we have faith, hope, and we know that God loves us.

We also know that the Lord is good (Psalm 106:1; 107:1; 118:1,29; 136:1) and that He, with power (as described in Ephesians 1:19-22 NASB) of *surpassing greatness that He has toward us who believe,* the *mighty power* (KJV) that raised Christ *from the dead, and seated Him at His right hand in the heavenly places, far above...every name that is named* and *put all things in subjection under His feet...* (NASB) is working for us!

...If God is for us, who can be against us?
Romans 8:31 NIV

For the eyes of the LORD run to and fro throughout the whole earth, to show Himself strong on behalf of those whose heart is loyal to Him....

2 Chronicles 16:9 NKJV

Keep your eyes on your standard, Jesus, with Whom — as a child of God — you

are joint-heir, to receive the healing God
has for you.

6

METHODS GOD
USES TO HEAL

God has provided many ways for you
to receive your healing.

One of the nine *spiritual gifts (the
special endowments of supernatural
energy)* (1 Corinthians 12:1) God works
in men by the Holy Spirit (vv. 6,11 NIV)
is *the gifts of healing* (v. 9 KJV). Notice
that the word "gifts" is plural. Healing
can come in many ways.

Sometimes people receive an instanta-
neous visible change in their body that
comes through the "power" and "inherent

ability"[1] of a miracle. This is another of the nine spiritual gifts in operation, *the working of miracles* (v. 10). The word *miracles* in this verse "is used of works of a supernatural origin and character, such as could not be produced by natural agents and means."[2]

Sometimes people receive miracles from God, but most of the time people receive healing from Him as part of a process. The meaning of the word *healing* in verse 9 is "a cure."[3]

God heals many people, and the visible change comes as a result of the process which takes time. In fact after you receive prayer, many times you won't notice any immediate difference physically.

You may not feel any better. You might even feel worse!

My husband provided an example that gives a clear picture of how it is that we can feel worse after healing has begun. If I fell down the steps one night and skinned my knee, my knee would hurt much worse the next morning after it started to heal than immediately after I fell.

After you pray or receive prayer for healing and you don't notice any immediate physical difference, just know this means that the healing power is working in your body. Concentrate on taking the medicine your Physician prescribed, by attending to His Word on healing.

If a doctor prescribed medicine for you, you would probably expect to take the whole bottle, and possibly a refill, before you experienced or saw complete results. You wouldn't throw the bottle away if you didn't feel one hundred percent healthy after taking one spoonful or pill!

After praying for healing, at least give God the same opportunity as you would a bottle of medicine! Keep taking your medicine, the Word, and continue *leaning* on God in *absolute trust and confidence* (Colossians 2:5).

Attending to God's Words

Whether your visible healing comes through a process or you receive a miracle, it is important to know how to attend to God's words. If you receive a miracle, you need to know how to keep it!

Some people lose the miracles they receive in healing meetings because they go home without knowing what to do to keep them. They need to know how to attend to God's words. As we saw, Proverbs 4:20,21 tells us to incline our ears to God's sayings, to let them not depart from our eyes and to keep them in the midst of our heart. Joshua 1:8 tells us to meditate on the Word.

We can attend to God's Word through hearing, reading and speaking it. You may want to listen to teaching tapes on healing or listen over and over to healing Scriptures on tape. It's a good idea, also, to read the healing Scriptures aloud yourself. You may want to buy a couple of good books on healing. Meditate on Isaiah chapter 53 to gain an understanding of what Jesus did to obtain healing for us. Then, **simply believe!**

They **Shall** Recover

Mark 16:17,18 describes a method God uses to heal, the laying on of hands, one of the signs that will follow those who believe. This Scripture shows us the confidence we can have in knowing the healing power is working in our bodies after we receive prayer for our healing. It tells us that once hands are laid on the sick, they *shall* recover.

And these signs shall follow them that believe;
In my name...they shall lay hands on the sick,
and they shall recover (KJV).

Verse 18 is worded ...*they shall recover,*
not "they *may* recover" or "it is *hoped*
they will recover." If you feel worse after
God's Word was prayed for your healing,
whether laying on of hands was used or
another of God's methods, keep your
confidence in Isaiah 55:11. When God's
Word is spoken it *shall accomplish* and
prosper in the thing for which it was sent.

In James 5:14,15 (below) we read of
other methods God uses to heal.

The Lord Will Restore the Sick

Is anyone among you sick? He should call in
the church elders (the spiritual guides). And

they should pray over him, anointing him
with oil in the Lord's name.
And the prayer [that is] of faith will save him
who is sick, and the Lord will restore him; and
if he has committed sins, he will be forgiven.

Notice that James chapter 5 instructs those who are sick to seek prayer. For God to include this instruction in the Bible is another strong indication of His willingness to heal!

In Bible times the sick called for the elders in the church to pray for them. We can understand the term "elders" to refer to the spiritually mature. If you are in a situation in which you are sick but are unable to locate someone who functions under the title of "elder," this verse does not mean you should go without prayer.

If I feel sick, many times I ask my husband, who is spiritually mature, to pray. Call for someone who you believe has the faith to pray for you. Be anointed with oil, pray the prayer of faith in the Lord's name and you will be restored.

...The earnest (heartfelt, continued) prayer of a righteous man makes tremendous power available [dynamic in its working].

James 5:16

In Matthew 8:5-8,13 we read of another way God heals. A centurion asked Jesus to heal his servant boy, who was lying at the centurion's house *...paralyzed and distressed with intense pains (v. 6).*

The centurion said to Jesus:

...but only speak the word, and my servant boy will be cured (v. 8).

Then to the centurion Jesus said, Go; it shall be done for you as you have believed. And the servant boy was restored to health at that very moment (v. 13).

As did the centurion, we can take hold by faith of the inherent power to heal in the Word of God!

God's Mighty Power

Sometimes God's power is so strong, standing up in its presence is hard!

First Kings 7:51 – 8:11 tells us that after Solomon completed his work in building the house of the Lord and the ark of the Lord was brought in, a cloud, the glory of the Lord, filled the Lord's house, *So the priests could not stand to minister because of the cloud...(8:11).*

When Paul, formerly Saul, was converted on the road to Damascus *...suddenly there shined round about him a light from heaven: And he fell to the earth...* (Acts 9:3,4 KJV).

Sometimes in healing meetings, people who receive prayer fall over on the floor. We call this being slain in the Spirit, slain in the power of God. This is what happened to the priests and Paul in the Scriptures above.

Receiving your healing doesn't have one thing to do with whether you're slain in the Spirit. If you're the only one in a prayer line of people who isn't slain in the Spirit, Satan will try to get you to occupy your mind with trying to figure out why you weren't. Some people aren't slain in the Spirit because of their type of personality.

Remember, God is a Father and loves us. He doesn't do things to scare or hurt us.

God's Power Is in Jesus' Name

Philippians 2:9,10 (NIV) states:

> *Therefore God exalted him [Jesus] to the highest place and gave **him the name that is above every name,***
> *that **at the name of Jesus** every knee should bow, in **heaven** and on **earth** and **under the earth.***

Have you ever noticed that everything in this world has a name? Trees, people, bugs, buildings, streets, all our foods and all diseases have names. The name of Jesus is **above** every other name, and it contains so much more power than everything else in existence that every knee must bow to it and submit to its authority in all three realms — heaven, earth and under the earth.

Jesus Christ is:

> Far **above** all rule and authority and power and dominion and **every name that is named** [above every title that can be conferred], not only in this age and in this world, but also in the age and the world which are to come.
>
> Ephesians 1:21

There is more power in the name of Jesus than there is power in the name of cancer or in the name of a tumor, arthritis or heart disease. And God has given us use of that powerful name.[4] Jesus said:

> If you ask anything in My name, I will do it.
> John 14:14 NKJV

First John 5:14,15 (NASB) tells us:

*And this is the confidence which we have
before Him, that, if we ask anything according
to His will, He hears us.
And if we know that He hears us in whatever
we ask, we know that we have the requests
which we have asked from Him.*

We have seen that healing is God's will. And anything in God's will we ask for in Jesus' name, we will have the requests for which we asked.

If you are sick, it is God's will for you to be well. Speak the healing Scriptures in the name of Jesus, which is more powerful than anything else that exists, to that sickness, believing you are healed. Believe the sickness or disease will submit to the authority of Jesus' name.

7

FAITH AND PATIENCE BRING GOD'S PROMISES

When you've filled yourself up with the Word, or attended a series of healing meetings or a conference, it's easy to have full confidence that you've been healed when you haven't yet seen a change physically. But one morning when you wake up and you don't feel any better, you may be tempted to decide to give up. It is vital to receiving or maintaining your healing that you apply the principles taught in Hebrews 10:35,36 and Hebrews 6:11,12.

Hebrews 10:35,36:

> **Do not,** therefore, **fling away your** fearless
> **confidence,** for it carries a great and glorious
> compensation of reward.
> For you have need of steadfast patience and
> endurance, so that you may perform and
> fully accomplish the will of God, and thus
> receive and carry away [and enjoy to the full]
> what is promised.

One of the biggest problems people in the body of Christ are having today is flinging away their confidence before they *receive and carry away [and enjoy to the full] what is promised.*

One time when I was ministering to a woman in a meeting I was holding, I was suddenly impressed with a picture of her traveling down a road. When she was halfway to her destination, she turned around and returned to the starting point. Then she started off again and did the same thing: halfway down the road, she turned around and went back to the starting point.

Many people in the body of Christ do this very thing! They go halfway down the road to healing, then give up, fling away their confidence and go all the way back to the start!

Second Corinthians 5:7 (NIV) tells us, *We live by faith, not by sight.* Because we are called to live a life of faith, not feeling, we are to trust what the Word tells us, not in what we feel or don't feel.

If you are like me, there are times when you don't feel saved. But even when you don't feel saved, you still are. It's the same with your healing. You may not feel healed, but you are healed. The healing power of God is residing in your spirit.

Hebrews chapter 6 tells us to *imitate those who through faith and patience inherit the promises* (v. 12 NKJV).

> But we do [strongly and earnestly] desire for each of you to show the same diligence and sincerity **[all the way through]** in realizing and enjoying the full assurance and development of [your] hope **until the end.** In order that you may not grow disinterested and become [spiritual] sluggards, but imitators, behaving as do those who **through faith (by their leaning** of the entire personality **on God in Christ in** absolute **trust and confidence** in His power, wisdom, and goodness) **and by practice of patient**

endurance and waiting are [now]
inheriting the promises.

Hebrews 6:11,12

When you wake up that morning not
feeling any better, you can decide to
fling away your confidence that you have
received your healing. Or you can decide
to continue to lean on God in confidence
and patience, resting in the knowledge
that the great reward confidence carries
is yours: receiving and carrying away and
enjoying to the full what is promised.

God wants us to be diligent to practice
patient endurance and waiting in order to
inherit the promises. And everyone wants
to be able to carry away to the full what
is promised. Keeping fearless confidence
for healing when you don't see any

physical improvement, and may even feel worse, is not easy. The Bible doesn't tell us the way will be easy, but it does tell us that God will show us **the Way.**

Psalm 34:19 tells us that many evils confront the righteous, ...*but the Lord* (the Waymaker) *delivers him out of them all.* John 16:33 tells us we can be of good cheer because Jesus has overcome the world. Jesus said, ...*[I have deprived it of power to harm you and have conquered it for you.]*

With the Waymaker inside us, ...*we are more than conquerors and gain a surpassing victory through Him Who loved us* (Romans 8:37). Believing these truths will give you confidence. Before we ever encounter a problem we can have confidence that we already have *surpassing victory* in it through Jesus.

The answer to the question, "Do you want to be an overcomer?" is usually, "Yes!"

The answer to the question, "Do you want something to overcome?" is usually, "No!"

We want to be overcomers, but many of us don't want to encounter anything that we will need to overcome!

We must expect that problems to overcome will come our way. And in many cases overcoming them will be hard! But God will make us able. People who run from the hard places in life will spend their entire lives running. And they will run around and around the same mountains instead of making progress. It will take years for them to experience victory over something they could have dealt with fairly quickly if they had stopped running and faced it.

To receive the fullness of the promise you desire from the Lord, the healing you desire, you must be diligent to lean on Him in confidence *all the way through* to the finish. Hebrews 6:12 warns: *In order that you may not grow disinterested and become [spiritual] sluggards....*

Proverbs tells us that the lazy sluggard will not prosper in life. *The soul of a lazy man desires, and has nothing; but the soul of the diligent shall be made rich* (Proverbs 13:4 NKJV). The sluggard, too lazy to plow in the winter because of the cold, begs for food during harvest time

because he has nothing. (20:4 AMP, KJV.)
Because he sleeps too much, poverty will
come on him. (6:10,11.)

God does not want us to be lazy because
He wants us to receive everything He has
for us. And to do that we must be
diligent. Many people haven't yet
realized that overcoming hard things can
be fun. God put His Spirit inside of us so
we would be ready for every challenge.

When you reach the point of not
shrinking back from the hard places, you
will begin to soar like an eagle over the
mountains that come into your life. I've
gone *all the way through* some hard
times in my life and *through faith and
patience* I'm now *inheriting the promises*
in those areas.

Face the problem that needs to be overcome, and be diligent to go all the way through to the finish so that you will enjoy to the full the promise on the other side.

CONCLUSION

To live in the divine good health God has for you, keep the following points in mind.

First, Jesus bought healing for you with His blood. Healing is yours as a gift. You receive it with your faith. You can't buy or earn it.

Second, it is illegal for Satan to put sickness on you, but he will if you let him.

It was illegal for Satan to kill Jesus, but he was able to do it because Jesus let him. Jesus let him because He had a good reason — He was going to use Satan's illegal action to redeem the world!

It is important for you to understand that it is illegal for Satan to put sickness on you, and there is no good reason to let him do it.

Resist sickness and disease in the same way you resist the temptation to sin. Sickness doesn't come on you all of a sudden. You begin to feel little indications that you are getting sick. When those indications first come, your responsibility as a believer is to resist those at that time.

If a temptation came to me to go out with a man other than my husband, I would resist that with everything in me because I know I'm not going to do something like that. We need to resist sickness and disease with the same godly indignation because it's illegal for Satan to put sickness on us.

Third, it is important to continually speak the Word of God on healing in Jesus' name to our bodies. The water of the Word (Ephesians 5:26) that is alive, sharp and powerful (Hebrews 4:12 AMP) will continually wash our bodies to keep them free from disease.

PRAYER TO RECEIVE HEALING

Pray the following aloud.

Father:

I thank You for sending Jesus to die on the cross to provide salvation and healing for me. I thank You for the use of Jesus' name which is more powerful than any other name that exists. The name of Jesus is above the name of (name of sickness or disease) that is in my body illegally. In the authority and power of Jesus' name, that (name of sickness or disease) must leave my body.

According to Proverbs 4:20-22, Your words are health to my flesh, and according to Isaiah 55:11, Your spoken Word will accomplish and prosper in the thing it was sent to do. I speak that, in Jesus' name, by Jesus' stripes I am healed according to 1 Peter 2:24, and I believe that I receive my healing. I thank You that as my Father You love me and have provided healing for me as part of my inheritance. In Jesus' name, amen.

Healing Scriptures to Confess

Now confess out loud the following Scriptures — do so as often as you need strength and encouragement. Confess the Scriptures so that they apply to you. For example speak 1 Peter 2:24 (below)

over yourself by saying, "...by His stripes
I was healed...."

*Who his own self bare our sins in his own
body on the tree, that we, being dead to sins,
should live unto righteousness: by whose
stripes ye were healed.*

1 Peter 2:24 KJV

*Beloved, I pray that you may prosper in every
way and [that your body] may keep well, even
as [I know] your soul keeps well and prospers.*

3 John 2

*Surely He has borne our griefs (sicknesses,
weaknesses, and distresses) and carried our
sorrows and pains [of punishment], yet we
[ignorantly] considered Him stricken, smitten,
and afflicted by God [as if with leprosy].
But He was wounded for our transgressions,
He was bruised for our guilt and iniquities;
the chastisement [needful to obtain] peace
and well-being for us was upon Him, and*

with the stripes [that wounded] Him we are
healed and made whole.

Isaiah 53:4,5

My son, attend to my words; consent and
submit to my sayings.
Let them not depart from your sight; keep
them in the center of your heart.
For they are life unto those who find them,
healing and health to all their flesh.

Proverbs 4:20-22

Bless (affectionately, gratefully praise) the
Lord, O my soul; and all that is [deepest]
within me, bless His holy name!
Bless (affectionately, gratefully praise) the
lord, O my soul, and forget not [one of] all
His benefits —
Who forgives [every one of] all your iniquities,
Who heals [each one of] all your diseases.

Psalm 103:1-3

*He sends forth His Word and heals them and
rescues them from the pit and destruction.*

Psalm 107:20

*Saying, If you will diligently hearken to the
voice of the Lord your God and will do what is
right in His sight, and will listen to and obey
His commandments and keep all His statutes,
I will put none of the diseases upon you which
I brought upon the Egyptians, for I am the
Lord Who heals you.*

Exodus 15:26

*And He went about all Galilee, teaching in
their synagogues and preaching the good news
(Gospel) of the kingdom, and healing every
disease and every weakness and infirmity
among the people.*
*So the report of Him spread throughout all
Syria, and they brought Him all who were
sick, those afflicted with various diseases and
torments, those under the power of demons,*

and epileptics, and paralyzed people, and He
healed them.

Matthew 4:23,24

And thus He fulfilled what was spoken by the
prophet Isaiah. He Himself took [in order to
carry away] our weaknesses and infirmities
and bore away our diseases.

Matthew 8:17

And behold, a woman who had suffered
from a flow of blood for twelve years came
up behind Him and touched the fringe of
His garment;
For she kept saying to herself, If I only touch
His garment, I shall be restored to health.
Jesus turned around and, seeing her, He said,
Take courage, daughter! Your faith has made
you well. And at once the woman was restored
to health

Matthew 9:20-22

And these attesting signs will accompany those who believe: in my name they will drive out demons; they will speak in new languages; They will pick up serpents; and [even] if they drink anything deadly, it will not hurt them; they will lay their hands on the sick, and they will get well.

Mark 16:17,18

Is anyone among you sick? He should call in the church elders (the spiritual guides). And they should pray over him, anointing him with oil in the Lord's name.
And the prayer [that is] of faith will save him who is sick, and the Lord will restore him; and if he has committed sins, he will be forgiven. Confess to one another therefore your faults (your slips, your false steps, your offenses, your sins) and pray [also] for one another, that you may be healed and restored [to a spiritual tone of mind and heart].

The earnest (heartfelt, continued) prayer of a righteous man makes tremendous power available [dynamic in its working].

James 5:14-16

PRAYER FOR A PERSONAL RELATIONSHIP WITH THE LORD

God wants you to receive His free gift of salvation. Jesus wants to save you and fill you with the Holy Spirit more than anything. If you have never invited Jesus, the Prince of Peace, the Healer, to be your Lord and Savior, I invite you to do so now. Pray the following prayer, and if you are really sincere about it, you will experience a new life in Christ.

Father,

You loved the world so much, You gave Your only begotten Son to die for our sins so that whoever believes in Him will not perish, but have eternal life.

Your Word says we are saved by grace through faith as a gift from You. There is nothing we can do to earn salvation.

I believe and confess with my mouth that Jesus Christ is Your Son, the Savior of the world. I believe He died on the cross for me and bore all of my sins, paying the price for them. I believe in my heart that You raised Jesus from the dead.

I ask You to forgive my sins. I confess Jesus as my Lord. According to Your Word, I am saved and will spend eternity with

You! Thank You, Father. I am so grateful!
In Jesus' name, amen.

See John 3:16; Ephesians 2:8,9; Romans
10:9,10; 1 Corinthians 15:3,4; 1 John 1:9;
4:14-16; 5:1,12,13.

ENDNOTES

Chapter 1

[1] James E. Strong, "Hebrew and Chaldee Dictionary," in *Strong's Exhaustive Concordance of the Bible* (Nashville: Abingdon, 1890), p. 73, entry #4832, s.v. "health," Proverbs 4:22: "...properly, *curative,* i.e. literally (concretely) a *medicine,* or (abstractly) a *cure;* figuratively (concretely) *deliverance,* or (abstractly) *placidity....*" (Abbreviations have been spelled out in this and in all other endnotes from Strong.)

[2] Isaac Leesser, *Twenty-Four Books of the Holy Scriptures Carefully Translated After the Best Jewish Authorities,* (New York: Hebrew Publishing Company, n.d.), p. 115.

Chapter 2

[1] Strong, "Greek Dictionary of the New Testament," p. 70, entry #4982, s.v. "saved," 1 Timothy 2:4, Romans 10:9; "whole," Matthew 9:22.

W.E. Vine, *Vine's Complete Expository Dictionary of Old and New Testament Words* (Nashville: Thomas Nelson Inc., 1984), "An Expository Dictionary of New Testament Words," p. 674, s.v. "WHOLE (made), WHOLLY, WHOLESOME," B. Verbs. 2. "*sozo*...e.g., *Matt. 9:21, 22* (twice)...."

[2] Vine, "New Testament Words," p. 547, s.v. "SAVE, SAVING," A. Verbs. 1. "*sozo* (...4982), 'to save,' is used (as with the noun *soteria,* 'salvation,') (a) of material and temporal *deliverance* from danger, suffering, etc. e.g....*from sickness, Matt.*

9:22, 'made...whole' (RV marg., 'saved')...
(b) of the spiritual and eternal salvation granted immediately by God to those who believe on the Lord Jesus Christ, e.g.,...1 Tim. 2:4."

Chapter 3

[1] Strong, "Hebrew Dictionary," p. 12, entry #403, s.v. "surely," Isaiah 53:4: *"firmly;* figuratively, *surely;* also (adversely) *but:* — but, certainly, nevertheless, surely, truly, verily."

[2] William D. Edwards, MD; Wesley J. Gabel, MDiv; Floyd E. Hosmer, MS, AMI, "On the Physical Death of Jesus Christ," *JAMA, The Journal of the American Medical Association,* (March 21, 1986), Vol. 255, no. 11, p. 1457.

³ JAMA, p. 1457.

⁴ JAMA, p. 1458.

Also, *MATTHEW HENRY'S COMMENTARY ON THE WHOLE BIBLE: New Modern Edition,* "Isaiah 53:4-9, The Humiliation of the Messiah," Electronic Database, copyright © 1991 by Hendrickson Publishers, Inc. Used by permission. All rights reserved.

⁵ Cross reference for 1 Corinthians 15:3 per NASB (1960, 1962, 1963, 1968, 1971) and AMP.

Chapter 4

¹ *The American Heritage® Dictionary of the English Language, Third Edition,* copyright © 1992 by Houghton Mifflin Company, s.v. "limpet." Electronic version licensed from InfoSoft International,

Chapter 5

[1] *Nelson's Illustrated Bible Dictionary,* copyright © 1986 by Thomas Nelson Publishers, s.v. "THORN IN THE FLESH." All rights reserved. Used by permission.

[2] *Matthew Henry's Commentary,* s.v. "2 Corinthians 12:1-10." Used by permission. All rights reserved.

Chapter 6

[1] Vine, "New Testament Words," p. 412, s.v. "miracles," 1 Corinthians 12:10.

[2] Vine, "miracles."

[3] Strong, "Greek Dictionary," p. 37, entry #2386, s.v. "healing," 1 Corinthians 12:9: "a cure (the effect): — healing." From p. 37, entry #2390 "...to *cure* (literally or figuratively): — heal, make whole."

[4] My teaching, "His Glorious Name," (available on audiocassette and video tape) contains detailed information on this subject.

REFERENCES

About the Author

Joyce Meyer has been teaching the Word of God since 1976 and in full-time ministry since 1980. Previously the associate pastor at Life Christian Church in St. Louis, Missouri, she developed, coordinated, and taught a weekly meeting known as "Life In The Word." After more than five years, the Lord brought it to a conclusion, directing her to establish her own ministry and call it *"Life In The Word, Inc."*

Now, her *Life In The Word* radio and television broadcasts are seen and heard by millions across the United States and throughout the world. Joyce's teaching tapes are enjoyed internationally, and she travels extensively conducting *Life In The Word* conferences.

Joyce and her husband, Dave, the business administrator at *Life In The Word,* have been married for over 35 years. They reside in St. Louis, Missouri, and are the parents of four children. All four children are married and, along with their spouses, work with Dave and Joyce in the ministry.

Believing the call on her life is to establish believers in God's Word, Joyce says, "Jesus died to set the captives free, and far too many Christians have little or no victory in their daily lives." Finding herself in the same situation many years ago and having found freedom to live in victory through applying God's Word,

Joyce goes equipped to set captives free and to exchange ashes for beauty. She believes that every person who walks in victory leads many others into victory. Her life is transparent, and her teachings are practical and can be applied in everyday life.

Joyce has taught on emotional healing and related subjects in meetings all over the country, helping multiplied thousands. She has recorded more than 225 different audiocassette albums and over 100 videos. She has also authored 51 books to help the body of Christ on various topics.

Her "Emotional Healing Package" contains over 23 hours of teaching on the subject. Albums included in this package are: "Confidence"; "Beauty for Ashes" (includes Joyce's teaching notes); "Managing Your Emotions"; "Bitterness, Resentment, and Unforgiveness"; "Root of Rejection"; and a 90-minute Scripture/music tape titled "Healing the Brokenhearted."

Joyce's "Mind Package" features five different audio tape series on the subject of the mind. They include: "Mental Strongholds and Mindsets"; "Wilderness Mentality"; "The Mind of the Flesh"; "The Wandering, Wondering Mind"; and "Mind, Mouth, Moods, and Attitudes." The package also contains Joyce's powerful book, *Battlefield of the Mind*. On the subject of love she has three tape series titled "Love Is..."; "Love:

The Ultimate Power"; and "Loving God, Loving Yourself, and Loving Others," and a book titled *Reduce Me to Love*.

Write to Joyce Meyer's office for a resource catalog and further information on how to obtain the tapes you need to bring total healing to your life.

To contact the author write:

Joyce Meyer Ministries
P. O. Box 655
Fenton, Missouri 63026

or call: (636) 349-0303

Internet Address: www.joycemeyer.org

*Please include your testimony or help
received from this book when you write.
Your prayer requests are welcome.*

To contact the author
in Canada, please write:

Joyce Meyer Ministries Canada, Inc.
Lambeth Box 1300
London, ON N6P 1T5

or call: (636) 349-0303

In Australia, please write:

Joyce Meyer Ministries-Australia
Locked Bag 77
Mansfield Delivery Centre
Queensland 4122

or call: 07 3349 1200

In England, please write:

Joyce Meyer Ministries
P. O. Box 1549
Windsor
SL4 1GT

or call: (0) 1753-831102

BOOKS BY JOYCE MEYER

"Me and My Big Mouth!"

"Me and My Big Mouth!" Study Guide

Prepare to Prosper

Do It! Afraid

Expect a Move of God in Your Life . . . **Suddenly**

Enjoying Where You Are on the Way to Where You Are Going

The Most Important Decision You'll Ever Make

When, God, When?

Why, God, Why?

The Word, the Name, the Blood

Battlefield of the Mind

Battlefield of the Mind Study Guide

Tell Them I Love Them

Peace

The Root of Rejection

Beauty for Ashes

If Not for the Grace of God

NEW: *If Not for the Grace of God Study Guide*

By Dave Meyer
Nuggets of Life

Available from your local bookstore.

Harrison House
Tulsa, Oklahoma 74153
www.harrisonhouse.com

THE HARRISON HOUSE VISION

Proclaiming the truth and the power
Of the Gospel of Jesus Christ
With excellence;

Challenging Christians to
Live victoriously,
Grow spiritually,
Know God intimately.